Weathering the Storm

Book Seven of the *Coming Back to Cornwall* series

Katharine E. Smith

HEDDON PUBLISHING

www.heddonpublishing.com
www.facebook.com/heddonpublishing
@PublishHeddon

Katharine E. Smith is a writer, editor and publisher.

An avid reader of contemporary writers such as Kate Atkinson, David Nicholls, Helen Dunmore and Anne Tyler, Katharine's aim is to write books she would enjoy reading – whether literary fiction or more light-hearted, contemporary fiction.

Weathering the Storm is her tenth novel and a continuation of this popular Coming Back to Cornwall series, which was originally intended to be a trilogy.

Katharine runs Heddon Publishing from her home in Shropshire, which she shares with her husband and their two children.

For all my family

near & far

Weathering the Storm

The wind and the rain batter the windows, fuming and frustrated. Safe and dry on the opposite side of the glass, Julie and I stand, each with a babe in arms. Somewhere behind us, Meg is tucked, shaking, into the smallest space she could find, between the arm of the settee and the bookshelf. She's not a big fan of storms, our Meg; or fireworks, as it's turned out.

"Me down," Ben instructs, wriggling against me. He's strong and wilful these days, and not keen on being held for any length of time. Julie's Zinnia, on the other hand, is just six months younger than Ben but soft and compliant, happy in her mother's arms.

"Sam'll be OK, you know," Julie smiles at me then turns to watch Ben crashing two dumper trucks together. I see Meg's backside flinch, her tail tucked between her legs.

Julie moves from the window to sit on the floor with Ben, placing Zinnia down and trying to encourage her daughter to get stuck in. For the time being, Zinnia is happy just to watch.

I, meanwhile, stay where I am – peering between the myriad drops that run down the glass, as if I've any chance of seeing the town, or the harbour, or the sea. Perched up and back above the town, Julie and Luke's house has beautiful views on a clear day but that is not today. Today we have mist and rain and grey, grey, grey. It's April and I'm waiting for the promised spring sunshine, but so far this month has been showers, downpours, and now this storm.

Picturing Sam out on the offshore lifeboat, which I know has been launched, I shudder. I can't bear to think what it must be like to be out there, with that brave crew: renowned for being 'gutsy', our town lifeboat crew are known for taking risks where others may be possibly more cautious (though this view may be coloured by the immense pride the townsfolk have in their lifeboat crew, and perhaps other towns say the same about theirs). Sam has come back home with second-hand tales of fifty-foot waves and stranded tankers or super yachts.

I hadn't wanted him to join at all but I knew I couldn't stop him, and that I probably shouldn't try. His grandad was an RNLI man and now that Sam's mum, Karen, is involved with Ron, another Lifeboat Lifer, Sam has been intent on following suit.

It's actually been a bit of a relief in a way, that he has found something to capture his interest and passion since Sophie left to live with Kate in Devon. He's been – understandably – sad and missing his daughter like crazy. And, while I do understand, between Ben and his wakeful nights and work at Amethi, I am shattered. If I'm honest, there have been some nights I've been relieved when Sam's out because although he's as lovely as ever, he's often demonstrably unhappy and that unhappiness has been seeping into our evenings together. I know that's selfish, and I should be trying to cheer him up, but sometimes it feels like nothing will do that and I just need some time to myself, to unwind and let things settle around me. Now, though, I wish he was here. It's hitting home; the danger that I know is very real for those courageous men and women who give their time willingly and freely to help protect others at risk from the sea and the crazy, unpredictable weather.

I picture the grand orange-and-navy boat fearlessly pushing its nose through giant waves, the men and women on board holding on literally for dear life. Drenched by spray and the obstinate waves, as the wind keeps whipping the sea, conjuring up swell after swell. I imagine Sam there, keeping an eye out for a stranded vessel; watchful for a flare to help them find their way. But how will they be able to see anything when even up here, on land, visibility must be less than ten metres? I can almost feel the whip of the wind and rain on my skin. How cold it must be out on the sea right now. I pull my cardigan around me and turn to the cosy living room scene, so at odds with the wild and wilful weather outside.

Julie is now pushing a car along the floor, Ben pushing his super train, which for some reason he's called Bernard, along in front.

"I'm going to beat you, Benny boy," Julie's saying.

"No!" Ben giggles.

Zinnia, meanwhile, looks placidly on.

"Some weekend this is," I grumble. I move to the settee and I reach my hand down to stroke Meg's trembling flank. Poor girl.

Julie sits back on her heels, waving her car at Zinnia. "You're meant to be playing with this," she says, then looks at me. "Not the best, is it? But it's bound to get better soon. Summer's on its way."

"I know. And then we'll be so busy."

"And that's a bad thing?"

"No," I grudgingly admit, "but I've been looking forward to this weekend. And now the weather's rubbish and Sam's somewhere out there." I gesture towards the window.

"And soon he'll be back, and that'll blow over, and you two can have your night out as planned. We'll be OK, won't we, Ben?"

"Yeah!" Ben says.

"Won't we, Zinnia?"

Zinnia stays quiet, looking longingly at her mum but not moving an inch.

"Come on, girl. You can move yourself, you know."

She won't. She could, but she won't. She'll wait for Julie to come back to her, and pick her up. Julie isn't sure if this is due to her daughter's less-than-ideal start in life or whether she's just got an incredibly lazy baby. She sighs and moves back to the girl who she worships, and falls at her feet, tickling the tiny sausage-toes until she gets a giggle. Ben, meanwhile, takes this as an open invitation to jump on Julie's back.

"Oof! You little…!"

"Ben!" I stand and scoop him up. "You mustn't do that. You'll hurt Auntie Julie, and then Mummy and Daddy won't be able to go out tonight."

"Thanks for the sympathy," my friend says, her voice muffled by the carpet.

"Any time." I carry Ben back to the window. "Daddy's out there, somewhere."

We look together and I rub at the window with my sleeve, although I know it's futile. Ben predictably wriggles from my grip once more. I sigh and rest my forehead against the glass. Why is Sam so bloody great that he's happy to risk his life for strangers? Why couldn't I have found somebody just a little more selfish?

But is that the slightest hint of blue I can see, out there? And have the rain and the wind softened just a little? I hope that the rescue has been a success and that the lifeboat, and whoever it is they've been saving, will be back on dry land, safe and sound, just as soon as can be.

Thankfully, and luckily for me, Sam is only in training and there's no way they'd have let him out on that boat. He's just gone down to the station to see if he can help. So, unless he's been swept off the harbourside by a freak wave, or been run over, or some other everyday accident has befallen him, I'm pretty sure he's going to be OK.

1

"So," Sam says, and smiles. I feel a relief flood through me at that smile.

"So…"

"This is weird."

"But nice?"

"Definitely. Weird but nice. It feels like the first time we've been on our own for ages."

"Because it is."

Since having Ben, and then moving in with Julie, Luke and Zinnia, our 'quality time' as a couple has completely disappeared. In the evenings, when the kids are in bed, we've fallen into a comfortable habit of watching TV, with Julie, and Luke when he's not away in London or India. Meg will manage to creep between us, creating a physical barrier, and when Luke is away it feels all the more important to spend time with Julie, although she's never said she's particularly lonely. I know what a culture shock it's been to her, though, to become a mum; and not to a newborn but to a one-year-old. She's had to find a way to bond with Zinnia, and vice versa. I suspect it could be a very lonely situation sometimes if Sam and I weren't around.

But tonight is about us, not Julie. Still…

"Shall I just give Julie a call, or a text? Make sure everything's OK?"

"No!" Sam puts his hand on mine, his laughing eyes on me. "Julie will let us know if there's a problem. Come on, drink up. Let's go and get something to eat."

"Yes, sir," I say, and I finish off the last of my delicious gin & tonic, letting Sam take me by the hand, collecting our empty glasses with the other and putting them on the bar.

"Have a good night," Andrew says. "Remind me I need to take Becky out sometime."

"Bit tricky when you're here every night!"

"Yeah, right. I need to sort something out."

"Good luck with that!"

I wave at Andrew with my free hand and then Sam and I are on the beach. It's dark already, the clocks only very recently having sprung forward, but still there's that hint of summer on the air. A little promise on the breeze. It's impossible to believe this is the same day as earlier, when the storm looked like it had moved in for good. As we press our footprints firmly into the sand, I stop and take Sam's other hand so that we are facing each other.

"This is nice."

"It is." He nuzzles my cheek, finds my mouth and kisses me. I close my eyes; breathe him in, and the warm, soft spice of his familiar aftershave, mingling with the subtle salt of the sea on the air. We kiss for a long time. I feel his hand on the small of my back, pressing me to him.

"Why didn't we get our own place?" he groans.

"Without Ben?"

"Well… no, but he'll be in bed by now. I wish we were, too."

"Not much room in that toddler bed for the three of us."

"*Our* bed, you idiot." He smiles again. It's nice to see him relaxed. When he came back from the lifeboat station this afternoon he had seemed buoyed up. Exhilarated. It had indeed been a successful rescue and Sam had sat in the radio room, listening in and familiarising himself with the terms they use. Also making cups of tea and generally being nice to have around.

I know he was partly so excited because he was picturing

himself out there. It will appeal to his sense of adventure, I know, as well as to his desire to help others. But one thing which may be in my favour, as somebody who isn't one hundred per cent sold on the idea of her fiancé risking his life on the stormy seas, is that we will really need to live within a mile of the lifeboat station, for Sam to be on the crew. And while we are close enough at the moment, at Julie and Luke's, we are saving for our own place. It seems unlikely that we will be able to afford anywhere in that radius and, although I'd love to, there's a slight silver lining if it means Sam won't be able to put himself in such ready danger. I have not voiced that thought to Sam, of course.

I kiss him again. "I'm starving," I whisper in his ear.

"I thought you were going to say something unbelievably sexy," he complains.

"Food is sexy."

"Not with your table manners."

He lets go of my hands before I have a chance to protest and he turns and runs into the darkness. I follow, as best I can, just barely able to make out his shape. It's hard going, running across the sand, but it feels good. I know this beach so well anyway, I don't need to see him to know where he's headed, and I reach the slipway just after he does. We both stand panting, bent over to catch our breath.

"Are we getting old?" he mock-wheezes.

"Maybe. Or perhaps we're just very tired."

"Or both."

"Or both," I agree, and he takes my hand and leads me up into the quiet, twisting streets, towards the harbourside restaurant where our table awaits us.

With a window table that was freely available to book – but which very soon will be reserved weeks in advance –

Sam and I sit in companionable silence for a while. Outside is an uninterrupted view of the harbour, obediently still and placid in the darkness; boats barely moving, rocking ever so slightly on the gentle water, their shapes silhouetted against the lights from the long stone pier; the sky and the sea a matching shade of deep, dark blue. It's too cloudy for stars right now, and too cold to have the window open. I sit back and consciously relax my shoulders, as I have to do from time to time. I feel like I spend most of my days walking and sitting hunched up – over a desk, over Ben, always at the ready for the next thing to happen and to leap to his aid should he need me.

"Alright?" Sam asks, and I realise he's been watching me.

"Yes," I smile. "I really am. It's so nice to have some time with you."

"You too."

"I can't believe that storm earlier, and the guys going out on the boat. Man, that was something." His face is lit up; animated.

"I know. I can't believe how brave those people are. Their families must be terrified."

"I don't know. I think they get used to it. They know why they do it. Trev's wife was there anyway; she's doing some of the PR work and social media, that kind of thing."

"And was she scared? For Trev, I mean."

"Dunno. I mean, I guess she probably was but she didn't show it. She was on the phones, taking calls from the local papers and websites, you know. It kept her busy."

"I guess it must have."

"I know you don't want me to do it, Alice," he puts his hand on mine. "And I know why."

I turn to him fully. "It's not that I don't want you to… well, I guess it is exactly that, in a way. I just can't bear the thought of anything happening to you."

"But it won't. Probably won't," he corrects himself. "And you don't worry every time I go out in the car, or up on the cliffs for work. They both have associated dangers, too."

"I guess."

"They do. And remember I had that RTA, didn't I? When I was a teenager. After you'd gone back home. It nearly killed me." He looks thoughtful. "So, I suppose what I'm trying to say is that bad things happen in everyday situations. And the training they give you in RNLI is excellent. They want us to be safe, and take every measure they can to make sure we are."

His face is so earnest. I can tell how much he wants this. And I love him for it. But it's one of my worst fears – possibly just after something happening to Ben. If I lost Sam, I have no idea what I'd do.

"I know," I say, and smile. Squeeze his hand. Look back outside into the dark. "That really was a storm and a half today. But look at it now."

The waiter brings our drinks across and we both realise we haven't even looked at the menus. "No worries," he says smoothly. "Take your time."

"Got to make the most of this, before all the emmets land," Sam grins. He knows how much I hate that term. Largely because I was an emmet – a Cornish term for a tourist, coming from the old English for 'ant' – and I still feel I have a long way to go before I can shed my outsider status. If that's ever even possible.

We both choose pizzas and, once they're ordered, sit back again. I take a sip of my wine.

"Have you heard from Sophie today?" I ask Sam.

"No." He looks sad.

"She's just busy, Sam. She's building her social life. I

remember it well, being that age."

"But I miss her."

"And she misses you. Don't think that she doesn't."

"Why didn't she come back last weekend, then?"

"You know why not. There was a party…"

"There's always a party."

"Maybe," I say. "And there will be more. But not every weekend. And we've got the week with her at Easter; that's coming up very soon."

"Yeah," he smiles. "Can't wait for that."

"And you've got the week off?"

"Yep, no worries."

"There you go then, you'll have a brilliant time together." I'm wishing I hadn't mentioned Sophie. It's a subject almost guaranteed to bring Sam down. But it's him who changes the subject.

"Listen, Alice, do you know anything about Jonathan and Janie?"

"Erm… no. Should I?"

"I don't know. It's probably something and nothing. Maybe even just nothing. But Janie doesn't seem very happy at the moment."

"Oh?" This is news to me. I see Jonathan at work every day and he seems OK. "Has Janie said anything to you?"

"No, not really. But I saw her at Mum's last week and she seemed pretty down. I did try to ask her in a roundabout way, if she was OK. She said she was, but…"

"She didn't seem it?"

"No."

"Want me to see if I can find anything out?"

"If you would, Alice. Like I say, it's probably nothing. She might just be missing Spain. I did wonder if she was doing the right thing, moving back here. But she and Jon seemed to really hit it off."

"They did, didn't they? But I do worry about her sometimes; he's so into his work and she's into hers, but her work is very solitary, isn't it? Stuck away in Soph's old room, in the glow of a computer screen."

"I know. I never thought my little sister'd be such a geek!"

"She must be good at what she does. She seems to have work queued up for her."

"Yeah," he smiles fondly. "I hope she's OK. I do like having her around."

Good, I think. He looks happier again. As our pizzas arrive and we tuck in, we fall back into that companionable silence. I realise I'm really hungry. And I haven't thought about Ben for about twenty minutes – damn, now I have. But it's OK. It's good, in fact. Sam is absolutely right. Julie would let us know if there was a problem. I roll my shoulders back again. Relax. It feels good.

Neither of us can finish our pizza and, as we set our cutlery aside, I glance at my watch. "It's only ten past nine!" I laugh.

"I'm bushed," says Sam. "But I don't want to go home yet. It feels like it would break the spell somehow. I know it's just pizza and a drink, but it's so rare I get to have you all to myself."

His eyes meet mine and I experience a little flip of my stomach; something I haven't felt for a while.

"I know," I say. "I wish we had the full night."

"We could go and make out on the beach." He grins.

"It's a bit cold…" I kick myself for being so boring. "What am I saying? Let's do it!"

We pay up and walk hand-in-hand, grinning, out into

the cold evening. Sam puts his arm around my shoulders and I lay mine across his back, my head against his arm.

It's cool but still out here and those clouds are moving away so that there is now the occasional star visible. With the fresh air, I feel a bit more awake, and I can't think of anything I'd rather do than go down to the beach with Sam.

We head towards the beach below the railway station. On the way we pass the old Bay Hotel, which is clad in scaffolding.

"Wonder who that belongs to now," Sam says. "It used to be the best hotel in town."

"Till the Sail Loft came along," I say.

"Ha! Yeah, I don't think they're in the same league somehow. No offence."

"None taken."

"This place has been here for years, and it's always been a hotel. Not like the Sail Loft and the others, that used to be people's homes. This was where the upper class would come to take the sea air, and swim in the pool down there." He gestures into the darkness; the nothingness and the knowledge of the steep cliff-face make me shiver, imagining the drop. "It's gone to rack and ruin over the last twenty years but it looks like somebody's spending some money on it now."

"I dread to think how much it will cost to stay there. And I bet it's got a *spa*," I say disdainfully.

"Hey, I thought you liked spas!" Sam laughs. "We enjoyed that one at Glades Manor, didn't we?"

"Well, yes, but that's in a different town. A different county, in fact, so it's no competition."

"Nothing is any competition for you, Alice Griffiths," Sam pulls me to him suddenly, and we kiss under a streetlamp. It feels very romantic. "Come on," he takes my hand and we slip down a little alleyway, between overgrown plants and hedges that spill out of messy gardens. Halfway down, we stop and kiss again and he slides a hand under my top.

"I thought we were going to the beach," I whisper.

"We are. I just couldn't quite wait."

He kisses me and I think of the Bay Hotel and the comfortable, expensive beds they'll no doubt be installing there. Still, with the sound of the sea just below and the feel of Sam's hand on my skin, I find I don't really mind where we are. Sam pushes me gently against the fence and we hear a dog bark. We look at each other and laugh then run the rest of the way down to the beach.

"Bloody hell!" Sam laughs into my hair, pulling me to him again. "I feel like a teenager."

"A very tired teenager," I say.

"Well, yes. But not quite so tired right now." He kisses me firmly, and he takes off his coat, lowers it to the sand. "My lady."

"Well, aren't you the chivalrous one." I sit on his coat and he kneels in front of me.

"I love you, Alice."

"I love you, too."

His hands in my hair, he kisses me again, more fervently, and together we move slowly down onto the sand. Above us, the clouds have cleared and the near-full moon is luminous. We're not as well veiled as we may have been under the cloud cover, and I can feel the cold of the night-time beach at the back of my head. I know my hair will be full of sand but really, truly, I couldn't care less.

2

Up at the Sail Loft, Mum and Dad are happier than I have seen them for some time. They had a small re-opening party in March, after closing for two months while they got the place in order. Sarah, who I met at the church baby group, has been absolutely brilliant in helping them redesign the interior – including the three rooms which now comprise their own living space. It's not a lot but, as Dad says, they do have the run of the house as well, and the private space of the office downstairs.

I'm so tired these days, I can't imagine sharing my home with strangers, which it sometimes seems to me is essentially what they are doing.

"No, we're sharing with friends instead," Sam said, slightly testily, when I voiced this thought to him. I think he's had enough, of the sharing; of the moving from place to place. And I agree, we need our own home. With a room for Ben, and a room for Sophie when she comes to stay. Except… what if we had another child? I don't know, if this is on the cards, or if it's something either Sam or I want. But even just from the point of view of having people to stay, I think we should have an extra bedroom. Which pushes us into 'four bed' territory, and that, my friends, is hard to find around here – in our price range, at least.

Still, Mum and Dad have settled into their new life, where guests come and go at all hours of the day and night, and a lie-in is a long-forgotten dream, because guests also demand breakfasts as well as beds. Every morning. The cheek of it.

As Mum says, "It's an early start, and then there's the cleaning to do – though we've got help for that – but then the day opens up, with some admin and keeping on top of orders and bookings, welcoming new guests, and gardening and all that. Without having to worry about dinners in the evening, though, it's really quite a nice way to live."

"I'm just glad you like it, Mum."

"Well, it wouldn't have suited me when you were little, that's for sure, but right now I'm really enjoying it."

This is a huge relief to me. I felt somehow responsible for my parents' decisions, firstly in moving down here – and when Mum was unhappy in her new job here I felt bad about that – and then for them taking on the Sail Loft, running a hotel, which they have never done before; although I never suggested that to them, and I remember feeling slightly put out that they were going to be taking over 'my' hotel.

Bea has yet to see the Sail Loft in its new get-up, although Dad's taken her on a virtual guided tour, via his laptop. I followed him around, nervously listening to Bea's exclamations. It's none of her business, of course; it's not her hotel anymore but somewhere in my mind it will always be her hotel and her approval matters to me.

I traipsed after Dad through the dining room – now painted a sage green and all the same furniture as before but stripped of the dark varnish, making the room lighter and airier. Into the hallway, which also had been a rich, dark space, and is now lighter, its walls painted rather than wallpapered – a change Sarah has made throughout. All the bedrooms are painted except for one feature wall, behind each bed, with a different wallpaper in each. My favourite is the one with the 'St Ives' design, featuring a pattern of rooftops much like those that can be seen through the window.

I loved the Sail Loft before, and I love it now. Whereas Bea's taste was classic and classy, Mum and Dad have surprised me by favouring Sarah's suggestion of something a little more modern, while still in keeping with the history of the place. In all of the bedrooms, the fireplaces that had previously been boarded up have been uncovered and restored.

All the bed linen is plain, crisp white. "It means it's easily interchangeable through all the rooms, and guests love a bright white duvet and sheet, as long as it's cleaned and pressed well, of course." This from Sarah. She really has done such a great job and Mum and Dad can't speak highly enough of her. In fact, she and Mum have become great friends, which is kind of weird. The three of us go out from time to time and we laugh a lot when we're together. I always feel good after a night out with them. Working with Mum and Dad has also opened some doors professionally for Sarah so she's now in a happier position of being able to work during 'normal' hours while the boys, Rory and Ethan, are at Goslings nursery, where Ben is – something she could never have done before. ("Trying to afford one child in nursery would be impossible – imagine trying to get the cash together for two of them.") With childcare vouchers, Sarah can now try to revive her career and the boys are loving all the activities at the nursery. "I do miss them, though – not to mention nap time. That hour or two each day was bloody lovely."

Meanwhile, Amethi is busy as ever. We've got a bit of a rolling plan now, with four yoga retreats each year and three writing courses. Then there is Jon's pop-up restaurant once a month. Aside from that, it is business as usual, with every self-catering week booked up over the summer and well into autumn. The Sail Loft is fully booked, too. We're busy, we're tired, but we're very, very happy things are going so well.

On Sunday afternoon, I take Ben and Meg for a walk, down to the beach. Ben is still small enough to need a buggy, as I learned to my cost when I ambitiously tried to get him to walk with me once. We have a lovely time playing on the sand, collecting shells and paddling in the shallows. Meg runs in and out of the waves, barking at them and leaping about delightedly with other dogs that come her way. The water is winter-cold so Ben and I don't paddle for too long, opting instead to move back and build sandcastles, decorating their crumbling walls with the shells we've found.

I love these times with him, when the world seems to belong to just the two of us (and Meg, of course). There are other beachgoers and the sea is populated by the shiny-suited surfers (a year-round feature) but there is so much space here. The sky is grey today but who cares? The air is fresh and breathes life into me, 'blowing away the cobwebs', as Dad always puts it. I pull a couple of bags of Mini Cheddars from my rucksack, and some bottles of water. Meg runs up and lies next to us, panting heavily. I pour some water into her bowl and she laps it up gratefully then turns her attention hopefully towards the Mini Cheddars. We sit on the cold, damp sand and I look out across the waves; the water is dark and grey today, matching the sky, and reminding me that summer is still a way off. It seems like even spring is still yet to commit.

I pull Ben back against me and he rests for a few moments; a rarity. He is not a boy who likes to sit still. I lay my cheek against the top of his head and I sigh. My eyes cast about for dolphins but there are none to be seen today.

When I think we've had enough, I spend about ten minutes convincing Ben of this then I manage to wedge him into his pushchair and brace myself for the steep walk back. Meg trots happily alongside, her lead really not a necessity, she is so well-behaved. We decide to stop in at the Sail Loft to say hi to Mum and Dad. They are happy to see me and even happier to see their grandson. We put Meg in the garden, where she's content to lie out on the grass and keep a watchful eye on the gulls that circle above, against the backdrop of soft, pillowy grey clouds.

Mum takes Ben off to their rooms to see if she can find a little treat for him – I have little doubt that she can – and Dad and I sit in the guest lounge, drinking tea and talking work.

Amidst the hospitality industry locally, there has been much talk about the Bay Hotel, which Sam and I passed the other evening. Nobody is quite sure who has bought it, and there seems to be an awful lot of money being spent on the place.

It makes me smile that Mum and Dad now consider themselves insiders, after taking a little while to find their feet.

"I don't know if it's an incomer or what," Dad says, "but Janet from the Bluebell says we need to watch out. They're adding rooms on and they've got a pool. She's keeping an eye on the website, which is under construction too, apparently. We need to know how they'll be pricing."

"I wouldn't worry too much, Dad. It's a very different place to the Sail Loft. It's probably going to be high-end boutique stuff."

"Hey, we're hardly low-end!"

I smiled, loving the pride he has in the Sail Loft, and how it now feels like it really is his and Mum's, rather than them tentatively caretaking for somebody else. "No, you're not low-end, Dad, but what I mean is, the Bay Hotel will probably attract a different type of client – they're bound to call them clients – to the Sail Loft, and to Amethi. Different people want different holidays."

"I suppose. Still, can't hurt to keep an eye on them."

When Ben starts to get edgy and grumpy, I am hopeful he'll have a sleep, and we say our goodbyes to Mum and Dad. Meg comes to my whistle – amazing, obedient girl – and I clip her lead on to her collar then off we go into the street, but I decide I'm not ready to go home yet. We walk along past my old house, which used to be Mum and Dad's, and David's before them. It's hard not to feel a little wistful when I pass by this place, which has seen so much of my life unfold within its four walls.

It's not like I can stand and stare at it. I hope that the new owners love it as much as I have done. I do stop for a moment, though, so I can check on Ben. Yes! He's asleep! I send Sam a message, letting him know I'll be a bit longer, and I follow the road down to town. The streets are already getting busier, with a steady flow of people on Fore Street, dawdling couples obeying the usual rules of stopping with no warning and narrowly avoiding an ankle-bashing from the pushchair. In the really busy months, I try to avoid this street altogether; though it's a shame, it's such a lovely place with its cobbles and cosily close-knit buildings. When I really love it is at Christmastime. Although it does become busy again, it is so twinkly and festive and I love the feeling of my coat and scarf wrapped around me (even though it's actually usually not all that cold and I end up overheating), clutching shopping bags, watched over by the star at the top of the church tower.

Today, I head determinedly along until I reach Joe's Café. I greet Emma and ask for a takeaway coffee. Check Ben is still asleep. Yes! I push him along the cobbles, which is no mean feat with just two hands to hold the coffee and Meg's lead, and also manoeuvre the pushchair. I reach the end of the street, turning left towards the lifeboat station. The boat is safely behind its huge glass door today and some tourists are taking photos of themselves in front of it. I smile and turn right, along the bare concrete walkway with its metal barriers to prevent anyone falling onto the rocks below. In stormy weather, the waves lay siege here, and I'd love to sit in one of the windows of the houses just behind, seeing the wild and angry waters rage and crash.

Today, though it is grey and not particularly warm, it is calm. I am happy to see that the bench I have been heading for is unoccupied. With Ben still sleeping on, his head falling towards his right shoulder, I put the brakes on the buggy and I sit, Meg settling herself under the bench. I take the lid off my coffee and blow on it. My first sip still scalds my tongue so I put the cup down, lidless, to cool.

And relax.

I breathe long and slow, thinking of Lizzie's direction in yoga. *Breathe out for longer than you breathe in.*

I gaze out across the sea, watching a boat leave the harbour. A cormorant stretches its wings on the rocks, fussing about before settling itself. Above, the ever-present gulls patrol the skies, watchful for unsuspecting holidaymakers with bags of chips or ice creams held far too trustingly open to airborne attack.

People pass by behind me but I pay them no mind. While Ben sleeps, I will rest, and take some precious time to myself. Maybe I'll check the estate agent windows on the way back. Though I know it's useless. Sam and I know everything that's on the market, and pretty much everything that's coming onto the market. We have eyes and ears around town, including Karen and Ron, who between them seem to know everybody and everything that's going on. There is also Sally, who Julie and I dealt with when we found Amethi. She has promised to tell us of any new places that might be right.

The thing is, I don't mind. I love living with Julie, and the closeness of our situation together. I have unrealistic secret imaginings of us bringing up our children together, like a little mini commune, but I know Sam is tiring of sharing, and I understand. I am determined we will find the place that's right for us. And with a bit of luck it will be too far from town for Sam to be able to be on the lifeboat crew.

I hear voices behind me. A loud, well-spoken woman. "I used to come here to Grandmother's when I was little but then Mummy and Daddy got the place in France and we never looked back. But then I saw the place here and I just felt drawn to it. Do you know what I mean?" She didn't wait for her companion to answer. "It's such a beautiful little place. And the history of it, with its artists. Not to mention the yachting community. It really has got everything."

You hear this kind of thing all the time. These are the people who have the houses in town; who can afford the places which Sam and I and a thousand other people like us would love but can't even look twice at. I smile to myself and shrug. It's just the way it is. As I hear her droning on, her voice still carrying as she walks further away, she actually stops long enough for her companion to say something. I recognise that voice. I am sure I do.

I turn to see their backs disappearing up the street that leads to the tourist information office.

"Lydia!" I call but she doesn't turn. It is her, I'm sure of it. Lydia, who used to be Jonathan's girlfriend; and the lovely waitress at the Sail Loft (between studying for her A-Levels and looking after her little brothers). She left for university, ended things with Jonathan, and never looked back. I haven't seen her in so long. But with a hot coffee, a dog, and a sleeping toddler in a buggy, I can't move quickly. I stand and call again but she and her companion have disappeared from view.

3

It's a beautiful morning as I drive our little red car – soon to be more rust than red if we're not careful – along the bumpy drive at Amethi. The wildflower meadows have been transforming over recent weeks, from dull brown stubble sitting grumpily just above ground to taller, greener stalks and stems, reaching tentatively, exploratively, upwards. Towards the sun.

"Morning, Alice!" Jonathan calls as I get out of the car.

"You're up early."

"Yeah, I'm… Janie's got some urgent work on and I thought it better to stay out of her way. And it's such a lovely day! It really feels like it might actually be summer soon."

"It does," I smile. I feel so much better than I have in recent weeks, and this is largely thanks to Sam's mood improving, too. That night out did us a lot of good, and I loved hanging out with Ben and Meg yesterday afternoon as well. A thought of Lydia flits through my mind but I push it away, remembering what Sam said about all not necessarily being well between Jon and Janie. I don't suppose adding Lydia to the mix would be helpful. Instead I say, "Fancy a coffee?"

"Yeah, I was going to suggest the same to you. I've got a few mini pastries left from the weekend breakfasts, too. They're a bit stale but a few minutes in the oven should freshen them up."

"This is where I'm supposed to say something like, 'Oh no, I really shouldn't', or: 'I'm trying to be good.' But actually, yes please I'd love that. I might even whip some of the covers off outside the Mowhay and we can sit outside."

"Steady on!" Jonathan laughs. "Let's not get too crazy."

We head companionably towards the Mowhay; the large communal area which adjoins the kitchen and is home to yoga classes, family parties, writing courses, and the occasional business meeting or away-day. When Julie and I first decided to make a go of it with Amethi, we'd thought we would target businesses a lot more than we have ended up doing. Somewhere along the way, leisure and enjoyment have becoming our number-one priority and while it's always nice to have a bit of extra income if a local firm wants to hire this space, I feel like it's better to keep business and pleasure separate. The hippy in me thinks that the good vibes soaking into the thick stone walls will be tarnished somewhat by stiff, boring meetings and presentations. Still, there are some lovely little creative, eco-friendly local businesses that we can cater for. We've even held a social function for the marine conservation charity Sam works for and that turned out to be a lot of fun.

Jonathan heads into the kitchen: "I'll make the coffee and bring the pastries out. You just sit in the sun for a while."

"If you absolutely insist," I say, and I move to the table closest to the meadows, easing the ties that hold the cover on then opening the table up to the elements. An early skipper butterfly flits past. "You'd better be careful," I murmur. It's not yet warm at night and that little creature is going to need to find somewhere nice and sheltered if the recent atrocious weather makes a comeback. Having said that, one look at the sky reveals calm, soothing blue, with wisps of clouds floating contentedly by.

I pull up a wooden chair and another for Jon, then I sit and try that rolling-back of the shoulders again. I know I have work to do but why not spend fifteen minutes appreciating this beautiful place? And besides, I can catch up with Jon about work so it's the best of both worlds.

"Here we go." He smoothly delivers two steaming mugs of coffee and a plate of warm mini cinnamon swirls, pecan pies and croissants.

"My mouth's watering," I say. "I've only had a smoothie this morning."

"That's no breakfast for a growing girl," he says with a terrible old-man voice.

"I think I've done all the growing I need to," I say, casting a critical eye at my belly, which has never quite returned to its pre-baby shape. Not that it was exactly washboard-flat back then.

"You sound like Janie," he says, and something about his tone makes me look at him.

"Oh. Do I?"

"Yeah, I... she..." he sighs, leans his elbows on his knees and his head in his hands, his sunny-morning brightness dissipated.

"Are you OK?"

"Kind of. Well, I don't know. We're not getting on great at the moment."

"Really?" I hope I sound suitably surprised.

"Yeah." His voice has fallen flat. "I feel like I annoy her, all the time. And it's like she's becoming more insular, with that job of hers, and she never really wants to do anything. I want to go surfing, or walking, sometimes; when I've got the time to, you know? And she doesn't mind me going, or at least she says she doesn't..."

"And you have asked her?"

"Oh yeah... she just says she never was into all that stuff. She liked it in Spain. Near the city. Art galleries, museums, that kind of stuff. Even the shops," he says with some disdain. "I just don't think I'm… this is… enough for her. I think she's bored and she's letting work take over everything. She loves it and it's like an escape for her. Only I don't want her to feel the need to escape."

When I picture Janie it is often this pale face, illuminated by the light from a computer screen. I don't say anything yet, though, remembering Sam's concerns for his sister. I want to see what light Jonathan can throw on the situation.

"And we work different hours," he continues after a moment, "and in different ways. I love working here; you know I do, but it takes a lot of time. It's not just cooking. It's not just prepping. It's planning, and sourcing, and pricing, and advertising, and… well, you know all this."

"I do," I take a sip of my coffee then nibble a warm, flaky pecan pastry. It is absolutely delicious and literally makes my mouth water. I look at Jon, encouraging him to go on.

"So, we live together – but we live where I work. Which isn't a problem for me," he adds hastily. "And not necessarily for Janie, either. She says she likes how quiet it is here, and she can just lose herself in her work. But I also lose myself in mine. And I do try to get out and keep busy; keep in touch with friends, and see Mum and Dad, of course. I suppose I don't like to sit still for too long. Aside from you and Sam, and Karen, Janie doesn't really see anyone but me. I feel like we've… lost each other, somewhere along the way."

I think for a moment. "I don't necessarily think you need worry," I say. "I mean, you say you think you're not enough for Janie, but she doesn't seem to feel the need for lots of people in her life. Yet she's chosen to be with you. And you two are in a fairly unique situation. When I was living here at first, I was on my own. So it was different for me. I was on hand for the guests staying here but I was also able to make sure I got some time to relax. I suspect you aren't getting enough time together and perhaps you're also not getting enough time on your own. You can't be."

"No. You're right. I must admit, there are times I would love an evening to myself. Seeing as most nights I'm working. Or a morning – just some free time, really. And it's not that I don't want Janie there but I haven't got any space. That's it," he says, glumly. "It's just a bit of a mess, really. I say I wish she'd do more stuff with me… but maybe really I just want her to do more stuff, full stop. Sometimes without me, so that she's got more going on in her life. I guess I feel responsible for her; for her staying in Cornwall when maybe she'd have been better going back to Spain. Living in Barcelona, or Madrid, or somewhere with a bit more of her kind of scene."

I hadn't really thought of Janie as having a 'scene' and to me she's always seemed fairly content staying here, and being at home a lot, but maybe Jonathan's right. Perhaps it's more that she doesn't really feel there is anywhere to go. Sure, there's the huge art gallery in town, and the sculpture garden… but things change slowly here. Perfect for the constant tide of visitors moving in and out; to them, these things are new. But if you live here, you do start to become aware that the only things which really change fast are the weather and the tide.

I love it, of course. I loved it even when I didn't live here. Maybe because it was a novelty to me, and perhaps I moved here at the right stage of life. But Janie left Cornwall when she was eight, and moved to a foreign country, with a different culture and way of life. Sam always says Karen dragged her there but then Janie grew up there. Perhaps that's at the root of her and Jon's problems. Maybe she just doesn't really want to be in Cornwall anymore.

The conversation turns to work and the forthcoming summer solstice, when Lizzie will be running her customary yoga residential course and we'll be wrapping it up with a solstice celebration, as the sun sets on the longest day of the year. I can't wait. These yoga retreats have become a favourite time for me. They are always in line with the solstices and the equinoxes and Lizzie brings her own brand of slightly crazy but very lovely paganism/hippiness to the event.

"It's a shame, in a way," Jon says, "that it's more or less the same people each time."

"I know, but it's kind of nice, too. And if somebody asks to put their name down for the same time next year, I'd be stupid to say no. In fact, I don't think I could say no!"

"You could say no booking until a certain time, then open it up to everyone – on the website or something. That's like some of these courses Janie does. They try to make them feel really exclusive, doing it that way. She says people are champing at the bit to get a place but in reality there are hundreds of places because they're basically online courses."

"Yeah, it's a bit different here, though, as we can only have twelve people anyway. And I feel like it would offend our regular people, if we said they couldn't just book again."

"I guess."

"What about your pop-up? Are you finding that's the same people time and again, as well?'

"Pretty much," he admits.

"Maybe we could open it up… say save one table to give away in a competition each month. Run it through the *Advertiser*." I'm starting to warm up to this idea. "It could be… I don't know, up to somebody to nominate a person they think deserves a nice meal out. Or ask the foodbank to put somebody forward. Or a local hero... Stop laughing."

"Sorry! I love the way this has gone from talking about your yoga courses to my restaurant, though. I do like the idea," he says thoughtfully. "Could we do it every month, though? That's quite a chunk from the takings."

"Let's add it to the agenda for the next meeting, and I'll mention it to Julie too so she can start thinking about it."

There you go. I'm taking my last sip of coffee, and I can head into the office having had a good fifteen minutes in the sunshine and fresh air and managed to come up with an idea with Jonathan, about how to make things a bit different around here.

"That was lovely," I say, "but now my desk awaits."

"No worries. And Alice, thanks for listening. I didn't mean to go on about me and Janie."

"I know. Don't worry."

"Things aren't all bad."

"I'm sure it will all be fine. Relationships always go through rough patches. It would be weird if they didn't, especially when you live together."

I think of Sam and his less-than-joyful mood of late. I'm grateful that this weekend seemed to cheer him up. I'm also glad I didn't mention Lydia to Jonathan. I suspect she's the last thing he needs right now.

4

On Thursday evening, Sam and I are off out together…
again. This time, to look at a wedding venue. Julie is
looking after Ben, on the understanding that she and Luke
will have a night out this coming weekend, when he's back
from London.

The place we're going to see was recommended by
Christian at the Cross-Section restaurant, when we
dropped in with Ben for lunch a couple of weeks back. "I
would love you guys to have your reception here but I
know you're looking to try and do this on a budget," he
said. "And when you know how many people you want,
and all that, I'll do you the best quote I can. But I thought
you might be interested in my mate's new place, up inland
a bit. He's just starting out and has ploughed a load of
money into it, but he needs some good reviews and
recommendations and I know this summer he wants to get
a couple of weddings in. Here, look," he pulled out his
phone. "The Longhouse, it's called. Apparently based on
an old Scottish design, or something. It's been built from a
kit. And he's plonked it right behind this bit of woodland,
so it's totally secluded. There's a clearing for weddings, or
you can have a marquee outside the main building."

Sam took Christian's phone and scrolled through the
pictures, from scrubland to building site to a fully formed
timber building with veranda and outdoor seating, with
freshly laid lawns and a small play area on the edge of the
woods. The clearing itself has been photographed with a
bower and seats, all set up for a wedding.

"It's beautiful," I said.

"It does look nice," said Sam.

"That's as much enthusiasm as you can hope for from him at the moment!" I'd laughed to Christian then turned to Sam. "It's got to be worth a look, hasn't it?"

"Sure," he'd almost shrugged but clearly thought better of it and said to Christian, "Thanks for the tip, mate."

"No worries. I'll give you George's number then you can arrange a visit. I'd be pretty quick about it, though. I know he's planning to give a couple of hefty discounts for the first couple of events but after that it'll be full price and I don't think it'll be cheap."

On the way home, Sam had been quiet. I could tell he was annoyed about something.

I had checked the back seat and seen Ben was asleep. I hate the idea of arguing in front of him but, unable to take Sam's sulkiness any longer, I had to say something. "What is it?"

"Nothing."

"OK." I waited a moment. "Should I give George a ring, then? See if we can make a date to visit?"

"Sure."

"OK." I gritted my teeth but rang George – who sounded cheery and friendly and said he'd hoped we'd get in touch. We agreed the date and time and I hung up. "Right," I turned to Sam, determined to be upbeat. "That's sorted. This is quite exciting!"

"Not to me, with my lack of enthusiasm."

"What…? Oh, Sam, I was only messing about."

"Well I don't really appreciate you taking the piss out of me to my mates."

"OK. I did think Christian was my mate, too. I know you've known him from school, but… that isn't the point, anyway… I don't get why you're so fed up. This is meant to be a good thing, us getting married. We should be looking forward to it, not falling out over stupid things. I know you're fed up at the moment, and I know you're missing Soph."

"Oh Alice, I'm sorry, I know I'm being a miserable git. But I can't explain it. I just feel like she's becoming so remote from me. And I am looking forward to getting married, I promise I am. And yes, this place looks brilliant. Thank you, for booking the appointment, and for keeping things going. I will snap out of this soon, I promise."

And he kept to his promise; if not snapping out of it exactly, he has gradually worked his way out of it.

It has helped that Sophie has called him this week and been WhatsApping a lot. I feel for Sam, I really do, but I suspect that even if Sophie was living with us she'd be gradually pulling away and becoming more independent. It's just the way it goes. She is growing up. And when I think back to that teenage girl who was missing her mum, after Kate left for Devon; and who had her heart broken by her first real boyfriend, I am glad for her, that she has found her feet so well and grown in confidence. Of course, I love her, but not in the same way Sam does – and I miss her, but not to the same extent. It is easier for me to be objective.

It's only eight miles or so from town but the landscape changes dramatically, from the coastal dips and rises interspersed with villages and pubs, campsites and B&Bs, to the rugged, flatter moorland where houses and farms seem more distant from each other and a huge sky stretches overhead, uninterrupted.

There is a large, carved wooden sign for the Longhouse, underlit so that it glows by the driveway, along an otherwise largely empty road. The drive is similar to Amethi's; i.e. not fully finished, and a little bit bumpy. The Longhouse is visible from the road and, like the sign, lit warmly. I can imagine it on a cold winter's afternoon, windows glowing tantalisingly and a long tendril of smoke curling up from the shiny metal chimney.

A small, smiling figure appears on the raised veranda, waving at us. He walks down the steps to meet us in the car park.

"Sorry about the drive," he says. "I'm going to get it flattened and gravelled, I think. Sorry, I should have started by introducing myself. I'm George."

"I'm Alice," I smile, shaking his hand. "And this is Sam. And don't worry about the driveway. It's very similar to the one at my place. Where I work, I mean."

"Ah yes, the famous Amethi," George grins.

I blush. "I don't know about that."

"In certain circles, anyway. Christian told me all about it and your award… amazing!" he smiles.

"Yeah, we were really pleased with that. We've had a lot of help from a great PR person. If you want her details, let me know."

"I might just do that," George says. "Anyway, I can't wait to show you around this place and I really hope you're going to like it. What shall we do first? Outside or in?"

"Shall we start out here?" I suggest, smiling at Sam and taking his hand. I am happy to feel him squeeze my fingers, and see his smile in return.

We follow George into the woods, down a path about two metres wide. All around us, I hear birdsong. It puts a spring in my step, as does the warmth of Sam's hand in mine, and the thought that we really might be getting closer to getting married. At last.

"I was going to put a wood-chip cover over this path," George is saying, "but my wife rightly pointed out that it will get in people's sandals and just be generally annoying so I might go with a crushed gravel that we can flatten, a bit like what I'll do with the drive. And we're going to have lights strung along the sides of the path, too. I did want solar but Imogen… that's my wife… said that would be no good during the day so I think we might have to have electric…"

I sneak a sideways glance at Sam. George is very likeable but extremely chatty. He goes on to talk us through the whole story of the Longhouse, and his Scottish and Norwegian heritage. Apparently, the design is a standard North European structure. And the woodland clearing is based on a place he'd seen in Scotland, where they hold pagan weddings and humanist ceremonies.

"I want this place to be for everyone, though," he says. "All religions, or no religion at all. Gay weddings. Trans. Whatever. People should be able to do what they want and everyone will be welcome here. Well, unless they're like far-right extremists or something!" He laughs. "Sorry, Imogen says I talk too much."

I'd be interested to meet Imogen, I think. She sounds very astute.

"It's fine!" I laugh. "And this is a beautiful place. I love what you're saying about making it available to everyone, too. It's how I think things should be."

"Yeah, I really believe it. And I've got an amazing chef lined up. I'm interviewing for staff… you wouldn't know anyone, would you? But I've got enough already to cover if you wanted to have your wedding, you know, this summer."

I look at Sam. "It sounds great, George," he says, "and I love this woodland area. But what if it rains?"

"Aha! I've thought of that. Well, Imogen and I have. We will have seating arranged like you might have seen on the website… in small sections, all around the centre, where the couple and the celebrant will be. And in the case of rain we will have gazebos big enough to cover each section."

"And if it's windy?"

George laughs. "You're giving me a hard time here! Well I know, this has got to be a hazard of outdoor events. In the worst-case scenario of weather like we had last weekend, we will hold it inside the longhouse. It can be done. I'll show you. If you've seen enough out here…?"

I look at Sam. "I think so. It's lovely," I say. "You're creating something very special here."

"I really hope so," George beams.

We follow him back along the path, again hand-in-hand, then over to the longhouse.

"We've got a ramp here for, you know, wheelchairs, and pushchairs, and for kids to run up and down! Have you got any kids?'

"We've got one. Ben."

"How old is he? Imogen and I are trying," he confides without waiting for us to answer his question.

"I… erm… good luck?" I say, and I can feel Sam stifling a giggle.

"Thanks," George smiles, holding open the door so we can go in.

It's beautiful inside and it smells of wood. There is also a fire going in a stove at the side of the room, though in truth it is very warm in here.

"I kind of regret lighting it," George says, his gaze following mine. "But I really wanted you to see it, because we can light it in the evening, if it's a chilly one, and it gives this really great light to the room when it's dark. And at the moment it's all set up as a restaurant, as you can see, but if the weather pushed us into holding an indoor ceremony, we can move things about. And we can have the bifolds open, if you still want an outdoor feel – though I wouldn't recommend it if it's really windy!" He stops and takes a breath. "We can do it, guys, if you'd like us to. I promise we will find a way through every eventuality and make it such a special day for you. But look, I'll let you two have a wander round yourselves now, and I'll give you some menus and some more information to take away and have a look at. Christian said he'd told you I'm looking to have a couple of early events, at a reduced rate, to kick things off here. I'd love it if one was for you two."

I feel like neither Sam nor I have got a word in edgeways so how he's come to take a liking to us, I have no idea.

"But no pressure," he says. "And now," bowing, and moving back towards the kitchen, "I really will shut up and I will leave you to it."

"Phew," Sam says quietly, when it is just me and him alone in the room. "Quite talkative, isn't he?"

"You could say that," I grin. "But I like him."

"Yeah, me too. And he seems to like us."

"Well, it's hard not to."

"Shall we look around outside again?"

"Yeah, OK. Let's go back to the woods."

I follow Sam out and he takes my hand this time. I feel a relief flood over me and an excitement, too. It's hard when Sam isn't happy and I suppose I have never really known him to be quite as unhappy as he has been lately. It is also exhausting, living with his less-than-cheerful mood alongside Julie, Luke and Zinnia. I feel like I have to put an extra-happy face on to try and balance out Sam's occasional gruffness. Although Luke has known Sam forever, and I know Julie loves Sam regardless. But I find it awkward.

We walk along the path, and I put my spare hand on Sam's arm, pulling him close to my side.

"Scared there might be bears?" he asks. "Or wolves?" He growls and turns to me, pretending to sink his teeth into my neck. Which turns into him kissing my neck, and slipping his arms around my waist. Pushing me gently back against the nearest tree and letting his mouth find mine.

"Ahem."

We pull apart to find George standing nearby. How did he manage to appear, just like that?

"Sorry, guys, I wasn't sure whether to interrupt or not."

"Probably better not to, then," Sam mutters.

"But I've got the menus and the pricing and all that," he proffers a shiny folder. "On all our new stationery," he says proudly. "Anyway, I'll leave you to it."

My face has turned red, I know it, but as soon as George has vanished from view, both Sam and I burst into laughter.

"Kind of spoiled the moment, that," I say.

"Yeah. Never mind. We'll carry on later," Sam says. "And it's getting on. I suppose we should get home to the munchkin."

"I don't think Julie would appreciate being called that."

"Ha ha. Very good. Anyway, I think it suits her."

We say our goodbyes and thank-yous to George, and get back into the car. I look back at the Longhouse as we turn onto the road then sit back happily in my seat. I have a good feeling about this place.

5

"Hi, Shona." I try to balance my phone between my ear and shoulder as I carry on skimming through the booking info for the solstice yoga, which is fast approaching.

"Alice! How are you?" Her warm Scottish tones hum into my ear.

"Well. I'm very well, thank you," I say distractedly.

"Paul's here, you're on speakerphone."

"Hi Alice," I hear the voice of the man I had dated for a very short while, before Sam and I got back together for the second time.

"Hi Paul. How are you both? Are you OK?" Ah… there's Julian's file. I knew it was somewhere. He was the first to book into last year's summer solstice retreat and the first this year, too. I've managed to misfile it. I'll just move it…

"We're getting married!" Shona's singsong happiness stops me in my tracks. I turn away from the screen. It is very rude of me anyway, not giving people my full attention on the phone. A bad habit.

"Wow! Congratulations, you two!"

When I'd been seeing Paul, he'd said he had no intention of getting married again. But clearly being with Shona has changed his mind. And I'm glad for them both. I always knew that there could be no future for me and him. He already has his family. Shona never had kids but has sort-of stepchildren from a previous relationship. Presumably, she and Paul are in agreement about what they want from life and, both being very successful – not to mention very good-looking – they are a perfect fit for each other.

"Thanks, Alice," Paul says. "Shona took me away to Paris for my birthday—"

"I missed your birthday!" I say, "I'm sorry."

"No worries!" he laughs. "I don't suppose I remember yours…"

"I was just getting to that!" I grin, genuinely happy for them both and hoping they can 'hear my smile' down the phone line. No matter how many years it is since my sales job at World of Stationery, I never forget to smile into the phone.

"I didn't propose," Shona adds, "if that's what you're thinking. I'm not desperate."

"I wouldn't have thought you were, even if you had!"

"But I'd been thinking of asking her," Paul continues the story, "then you know what Paris is like. The city of love and all that."

"Sure." I once went on a school trip when I was thirteen, with a load of other teenagers. I remember a stuffy coach ride, a ferry trip with no sleep whatsoever, and traipsing up the Eiffel Tower, as well as a whistle-stop tour of Le Louvre. Also a couple of hours where we were encouraged to explore a little, and all of us ended up in Burger King. A queue of British teenagers asking for "*Un Whopper, s'il vous plait.*"

"It was on the last night," Shona chips in now. "Sitting outside a restaurant. He got down on one knee and everything. We had a round of applause, and this guy with an accordion came and played for us. Once I'd said yes, of course."

"Or *oui*," says Paul.

I can definitely hear both their smiles.

"Well that sounds absolutely perfect," I say. "And I am really, really pleased for you both. Thank you for letting me know."

"Well, I'm a bit scared we've turned into a bit of a nightmare couple," Paul says. "You must tell us to shut up if we go on too much."

"We're just so happy!" giggles Shona.

"Honestly, I'm just delighted for you both. You should be happy. And you should celebrate life's high points, for sure."

"Thank you, Alice. We will have an engagement party soon. You and Sam had better be there, and Julie and Luke, and Sue and Phil, of course."

Shona has worked wonders for me and Julie at Amethi, and more recently for Mum and Dad at the Sail Loft too.

"We wouldn't miss it for the world." I am already wondering who could babysit Ben and Zinnia – and look after Meg. Normally, Julie and I take it in turns to let the other one have a night out. Not that it happens that frequently anyway.

"Great. I'll get the details over to you when we know what we're doing. But look, Alice, I did want to talk to you about something else as well."

"Oh?"

"Yes. And I just wanted to give you the heads-up. Look, I'll take you off speakerphone now so we can chat better."

"Bye, Alice!" Paul calls. "Catch up soon."

"Bye, Paul." Why do I have a sudden feeling of dread in the pit of my stomach? I listen to the *clunk* and *click* of Shona fiddling with her phone.

"There, that's better. And look, I don't want to alarm you either, sorry. But you need to know about the Bay Hotel."

"The Bay?"

"Yes. They contacted me to see if I'd handle their PR."

"OK..."

"They're hoping to make a big splash with a grand launch day in September, once the school holidays are done and dusted. I don't think families with kids are their chosen clientele."

So far, so good. "Right. Well, September's quite soon, isn't it? I mean, there's still scaffolding up and…"

"Yeah, I know, but the owner's pretty driven and she's got a huge team of people working on it all. She's confident she can do it."

"OK. Well, good for her." I'm not sure where this is going but I still don't particularly like it.

"Yeah, anyway, sorry. I can't really say too much, you know, from a professional perspective. But I do need to tell you that I won't be working for her. I think it's a conflict of interests, with me working for Amethi and the Sail Loft."

"Really?"

"Yes. I hate to tell you but I think they could be stiff competition for you, Alice. Like I say, I can't tell you too much but let's just say that the kind of things they'll be offering aren't too far from what you're doing at Amethi."

"But it's a lot more expensive…?" I say hopefully.

"I don't know about that. And I don't know if you're aware but it's going to be a mixture of self-contained suites alongside catered rooms, rather than a standard hotel."

"Right." This is not sounding good.

"There'll be yoga. And a dedicated yoga studio, and full-time yoga teacher."

"OK."

"And writing courses. With some big names, if the owner's to be believed."

"Shit."

"And then there's that pool…"

Of course. The pool. Now that is something we do not

41

have, as are the sea views. Still, we have an established name. We have loyal customers, some of whom have become friends. And maybe not everybody wants the sea views or the chance to swim in saltwater pool outside in one of the most beautiful spots in the UK.

"Don't panic, though," says Shona. "And I'm not trying to worry you. I just thought you might like to know what's happening. And I'm not a hundred percent on the pricing. But I wanted to assure you I will not be working with them."

"Thank you, Shona."

"No worries."

"But you can expect some fairly extensive coverage, I'd say, if they do get the right PR person. And I'm sure they will. She's from some wealthy family, and she's worked in the City. Used to come here for family holidays apparently so she's got some romantic notions about the place. Having said that, I can see her putting some locals' noses out of joint if she's not careful."

"Well, that's easily done."

"True!" she laughs. "I thought you might want to ring them, on the pretence of perhaps booking with them in the autumn. See what you can get from them in terms of pricing and that."

"Great idea. Thank you, Shona. I really appreciate you letting me know, and you not working for them. You should, you know, if you want to."

"I shouldn't! I definitely shouldn't. Don't you worry, Alice. I've got your back. And your parents', though I don't think it will be too much of a problem for them."

"You are a star. And I am so happy for you and Paul, as well."

"Me too. Thanks, Alice."

42

I sit for a moment, thinking about what Shona has just told me. Will this really be a threat to us at Amethi? You only have to look around the town to see how much holiday accommodation there is and how crammed the car parks and streets are during high season, and even before and after, when older with grown-up kids or younger couples with no kids yet make the most of the cheaper prices and the slightly quieter streets, pubs and restaurants. There is certainly no shortage of people who want to holiday here so hopefully the Bay will have their customers (I still think they'll call them clients) and we will have ours and there will be plenty of everything to go around.

Still, it piques my interest. I think I will give them a call and see what more I can find out.

I move Julian's file as planned and just double-check I've got all the booking info in the right place, then I look up the number for the Bay and dial it. I haven't really planned what I'm going to say but I can always hang up if I need to. Should I have blocked caller ID or am I just being paranoid now?

"Hello, Bay Hotel?" A man's voice – and a local one. Not what I was expecting.

"Oh, hi. I was hoping to speak to somebody to get some information, please. About pricing and what kind of things you'll be doing there, and…" I am babbling.

The man clears his throat. "Let me stop you there. I'm the site foreman, I just picked up the phone 'cos the manager's out on the scaffolding at the moment, with the owner. Hang on and I'll get her to come and have a word."

"Oh, sure. Thanks." I breathe deeply. I don't know why I've come over all nervous. I'm just a potential client, phoning to get some info.

I hear shuffling and a muffled conversation, as the man

has presumably covered the mouthpiece. "Here she is, love," he says, and I smile as I imagine that is not how the management of the Bay Hotel would wish their guests to be addressed.

I hear another little shuffling noise as the phone is handed over. Then, "Hello, Bay Hotel. Lydia speaking. How may I help you?"

Lydia? I freeze. Say nothing. Hang up.

6

"Shit," Sam says when I tell him and Julie what happened.

"Shit," Julie echoes in agreement.

"Shh," I say, darting my eyes over to the kids, who are both in their highchairs, happily occupied with mushing food onto the trays, Ben also choosing to drop handfuls of it over the side and laughing at the satisfying sound of mashed potato hitting the shiny kitchen floor.

"Ben!" I say and he looks at me and laughs again.

"So, Lydia's back?" asks Julie.

"Looks like it."

"Does Jonathan know?" Sam asks semi-gruffly.

"I don't know. I didn't mention I'd seen her." I realise too late I had not actually mentioned this to Sam, either. I try to backtrack. "Well, I thought I did. The other day. I wasn't sure, though."

Sam does not look happy. I haven't told him yet about the conversation I'd had with Jonathan, either. Sam is very protective of his sister; perhaps all the more so because they were so far away from each other for so long. Also, now Sophie's away, I think he's transferring some of his paternal feelings towards Janie instead. Now she's back and Sam's so happy to have her here, I know he doesn't want anything messing that up. I'd better tell him about it later, I suppose, but is that betraying Jon's confidence?

Oh, it's tricky when everybody is so close. It may seem all lovely and cosy, with my best friend married to Sam's best friend – and my chef (and friend) living with Sam's sister – but what if something goes wrong? I suppose maybe if you've grown up in a small town this might all seem quite normal. I remember somebody – I think it was Kate – saying about her ex being with a friend of hers, then the friend going out with his brother. I always used to think soap operas were unrealistic but, while a touch on the dramatic side, since I've lived in a small town I can see how people's lives do become more closely intertwined with others'. It is now clearer than ever that it is important for Sam and me to get our own place. I don't want anybody else affecting our relationship more than is necessary.

"So you didn't ask her anything?" Julie asks now.

"No, I was too shocked. And besides, she'd know my voice, wouldn't she? I can't believe it, though! Well, I mean it's obviously up to her where she works but why hasn't she been in touch to say she's living down here again? And I can't help feeling like she's using her knowledge of our business, for her own gain."

"Though the yoga and writing courses might be the owner's idea," Sam says, very fairly I think, considering Lydia's his sister's boyfriend's ex.

"Well, yes, maybe." I can't keep the note of cynicism out of my voice. "But it feels like a bit more than coincidence, doesn't it? That they're doing almost the same as us."

"As far as you know," Sam reminds me.

"Yes, I suppose. It hasn't been confirmed yet. But Shona's not going to be making it up, is she?"

"There's one way to find out," says Julie. She picks up the phone. "What's the number?"

"There won't be anyone there now," I say but I quickly Google the number and show it to her. "It's nearly six."

"If they're worth their salt, and they want to launch in September, they're going to need somebody to be taking calls," Julie says. "Shh…"

As I move over to Ben and Zinnia, to try and encourage them to actually put some food in their mouths rather than smearing it round their faces and every available surface, Julie says, "Hello? Is that the Baywatch Hotel?" in a very posh voice.

Sam pulls a chair close to Zinnia, grinning at me. He hands a chunk of sweet potato to Julie's daughter while her mum listens then speaks again.

"The *Bay* Hotel… so sorry. I was thinking of that wonderful programme, of course. I do apologise. Anyway, I am thinking about bringing some friends to Cornwall in October, on a bit of a girls' weekend, you know? We need some serious time away from the chaps, and I'd heard about the Baywatch on the grapevine … the grapevine, I mean word of mouth, not a magazine … yes, that's right. I was just wondering if you could provide me with some information. I heard mention of yoga, and an outdoor pool. Is the weather nice enough at that time of year, in Cornwall? I'm more of a Monaco girl normally…"

Where is all this coming from? I can't look at Sam but instead smile at Ben, as he mushes some food into his mouth, with a spoon.

Julie is not finished yet. "And we're looking for somewhere a bit… exclusive. But not too pricey, you know? I have a mixed circle of friends. One or two of them will have to foot the bill themselves … thank you … oh, that is rather reasonable. Rather less than I'm used to." Julie casts a glance my way. "Yes, yes, I see. Oh, I think that's a marvellous idea. Makes it a bit more… accessible." She adds a touch of distaste to this last word. "Alright then, my darling, thank you so much. I'll be in touch."

She hangs up, and then looks at me.

"Well?" I ask. I don't like the look on her face.

"Shona's right. Seems like pricing isn't too far from ours."

"How is that possible?" I ask. "That place must have cost a fortune, not to mention all the work they're doing to it."

"Standard practice isn't it, if you've got some money behind you?" Sam suggests. "Make a loss to start, while you build up your reputation. Bit like George at the Longhouse."

"But on a much larger scale," I say. "Shit. But also, we should decide what to do about that, Sam. If we want to go for it. Bloody hell." I want to think about the wedding… if it's going to happen at the Longhouse, we need to let George know soon. But we need to pay in full, to secure the deal he's offered. That's going to eat into our deposit on a house, if we ever find one. But now this, with the Bay Hotel is worrying away at me. Not to mention Lydia. What is she up to?

7

Sam and I decide it's best not to mention Lydia to Janie or Jonathan, yet. I don't like keeping secrets but there's quite a nice cosy feel to Sam and I keeping this one together.

Feeling on a firm footing, I decide it's best to tell him about the conversation I had with Jon. I wait till we're in bed, lights on and books in hand. I love this feeling, of us both together; lost in the separate worlds of our books but very much together. Tonight, though, I can't lose myself among the pages. There are too many trains of thought rattling through my mind. Most of them relate to Lydia.

"Sam," I say.

"Mmm?"

"You know what you were saying the other day, about Janie and Jon?"

"Yeah?" He turns to me now, one hand keeping his place in his book.

"Well, I did get a chance to speak to Jon… I didn't say anything to him about it," I add quickly. "He just opened up a bit."

"Right?" Sam is sitting straighter, alert to any threat to his sister.

"Yes. And it's nothing to worry about. From Jon's point of view, anyway."

"What do you mean?" There's an edge to his voice now and I'm already kicking myself for bringing this up.

"Nothing, really. Honestly, I think it's something and nothing. And you have to promise not to say anything to Janie about this as I am betraying Jon's confidence now."

"Hmm." Sam sounds displeased with Jon, though he really does have no reason to. And now I feel protective of my chef, and friend. He's a good man. He may have been a pain all those years back when he first came to work at the Sail Loft with me but that was a long time ago, and he's changed an awful lot since then. Some of these changes are thanks to Lydia but I am smart enough to know not to voice that particular thought.

"Really, Sam. He confided in me at work, and he's worried. And I think he's a bit down, actually."

"Why's he worried?" Sam, amazing and always decent human being that he is, softens at this.

"He thinks Janie isn't happy in Cornwall. And that he isn't enough for her. That this... what they have here... isn't enough for her. I personally think they're just going through a rough patch. And he's being hard on himself. But he might have a point. For your mum, coming back here is coming home. For Janie, home is in Spain, isn't it? She may have been born in Cornwall but she has lived a much larger part of her life in Spain."

"This has crossed my mind," Sam admits.

"And Jon... well, he was all set to leave Cornwall, wasn't he? He'd had enough. Then Janie arrived, and he came to join us at Amethi, and has thrown himself into his work."

"Janie works really hard too," Sam says, bristling.

"I know, I know," I quickly counter. "And that's maybe part of the problem... that both of them work so hard. And I'm starting to realise Jon can be quite up and down. I think he feels they've become detached from each other. She can work on her computer, in that weird nerdy world of hers–" I chance this to make Sam smile and I'm relieved to see it work. He knows how much I think of Janie "–but I think Jon feels like she would be happier back in Spain –

or at least somewhere livelier. More… cultured." I hesitate to say the word. Cornwall lacks nothing for me and has plenty of culture but this is the best word I can think of. "You know, with theatres and museums and concerts. She loves all that, I think, and there's not enough of it round here. Jon thinks it's making her withdraw into herself."

"He probably has a point," Sam says thoughtfully. "So it's not that he's not into her anymore?"

"No! Definitely not. He seems really concerned about her, and their relationship. My worry is that she has become a bit withdrawn and that Jonathan is starting to do the same. I do think he might have a bit of a tendency to depression, you know."

There was that time when I stupidly thought something had happened between him and Julie, that Christmas a couple of years ago. Back then, he'd been really down and ready to leave Cornwall, for something better, or so he hoped. He'd been a bit of a ladies' man when we first met, like he was always looking for something better. It took a while for him to settle into a relationship with Lydia and if I'm honest I don't think I've ever known him so happy as when that was going well. But of course when she left for uni, then London, and ended things, it hit him hard.

Sam looks thoughtful. "I wouldn't have put him as a depressive type. He always seems pretty chirpy. And everyone likes him. A bit too much, sometimes," he smiles and I know he's referring to Jonathan's looks, which have many of the guests at Amethi making comments. Women nudging each other and finding reasons to 'just pop over to the kitchen' with an extra request for dinner.

"I wonder if that's actually not much fun for Jon, sometimes. He's cultivated a very charming personality and he's a talented chef. But I think I know him well enough to say he's not as confident as his persona might suggest. And is it actually really annoying for really attractive people, that their looks are the first thing people comment on? It seems like it might be quite nice but actually perhaps it's disappointing. Overlooking all the other great qualities somebody may have."

Having said that, Julie – who draws admiring glances everywhere she goes – doesn't seem fazed by it. I am sure she used to enjoy the attention at times but she's also great at letting it wash over her. She's more intent on having fun than anything and she's always had a fantastically positive outlook on life. The only thing I've known to have made her really miserable is the hard time she and Luke had trying for a baby. And now she has Zinnia – she has found a solution to that problem, but it hasn't magically cured the pain she felt back then. It isn't as easy as all that.

Still, the point here is that maybe being incredibly good-looking can be both a blessing and a curse – for Jonathan, at least. Of course, all this is conjecture and maybe tells you more about me than about anyone else.

"I don't find it a problem," Sam says now, putting his arm round me. "I know people are drawn to my looks but I don't blame them. I find it very hard to walk by a mirror, to be honest."

"Yes, of course."

"But really, I feel bad for Jon, and for Janie. It's not easy."

"No, but relationships aren't. Or not all the time. They can't be. We've certainly been through a few bad times."

"True."

"I just hope Lydia's presence doesn't cause any issues."

"It had better not do." Sam is suddenly on the defensive again. He's so prickly at the moment.

"I don't mean for Jon. That ship has sailed, I'm sure of it. I was thinking of Janie. If she is lacking in confidence at the moment, or maybe even feeling a bit insecure… and I don't know if she is but it's possible… then it may not help, having Jon's ex on the scene. Not *on the scene* but, well, just having Lydia about may not be great."

"No."

"So let's keep it between ourselves for now?"

"Yep."

We've come full circle and while I hope I have helped Sam see that Jonathan is not a threat to his sister's happiness – I really hope he isn't – and that life is not all roses for Jon, I feel slightly ill at ease. As we both return to our books, I can't help wishing I hadn't said anything.

8

Soon enough, the Easter holidays are here and Sam's mood is lifted by the arrival of Sophie. For a whole, glorious week.

He goes to the station to collect her and when they arrive at the house I am struck, as I always am, by just how grown up the girl is these days.

"Sophie!" I throw my arms around her.

Ben, who was busy bashing a wooden spoon on a range of pans, stands and runs to her, hugging her legs. "Sister!"

She laughs, and extricates herself from my hug, giving me a kindly kiss on the cheek, then scoops up her little brother and swings him into the air. Sam arrives at the doorway, bowed down under the weight of his daughter's bags. "I thought you were just coming for a week," he pants but I can see the pleasure in his eyes.

Julie and Luke have taken Zinnia up to Luke's dad's for the day, judiciously allowing us some family time. I took Ben around town this morning, picking up all Sophie's favourite things: cheese and onion pasties served over the counter from the shop by the harbour; meringues from Browns' cake shop, and – far too early, really – strawberries from the deli, along with olives and sourdough bread, and a selection of salads to balance the scales a bit in terms of healthiness.

These are laid out on the table, in readiness for a family lunch before a planned afternoon at the beach.

"It's so good to see you, Sophie."

She has put Ben down and already has her phone in her

hand, smiling to herself while presumably replying to a message.

"You too," she looks up briefly.

"Is that Amber?" Sam asks.

"Huh? Oh, no, but I'm seeing her tomorrow. That is, if that's OK."

"Of course it is," Sam says. "I've got the week off work, we've got loads of time."

"That's great, Dad." Sophie grabs one of her bags and heads towards the room which is to all intents and purposes her own, when she's with us.

"OK, well, lunch is ready in a few minutes," he calls slightly redundantly.

"Great," comes the reply but do I detect a false brightness – as used by young people the world over when addressing their elder and therefore slightly less than worthy relatives?

I look at Sam. He has picked up Ben, who is doing his best to bash his dad on the head with the wooden spoon. "Don't grow up, son," Sam says.

I smile. "I think he's going to have to. But don't worry, they say boys mature more slowly than girls. I mean, you're going to have to grow up some day."

"I suppose. Ah, I guess I just want her to come and hang out with us," he says wistfully.

"I know, and she will… but she's sixteen, or close enough. And if we try to push her, she will push back. Just let her be. We've got a whole week with her. And this afternoon will be really nice."

It's true. The sun is out, the sky is blue, and the prospect of a few hours at the beach is immensely cheering. I miss those days when I used to be able to head down there alone… lose myself for a while amidst the waves then lie back on the sand, and doze. Actually have a little sleep. Nowadays, I can't relax in the same way, having a toddler to keep an eye on. And besides, he just loves being there, so much. Building sandcastles and helter-skelters to roll a ball down. Paddling in the shallows and generally having a whale of a time. This won't last forever, as Sophie's teenage presence reminds me, and one day I will have that time again, when I can swim undisturbed, and lie on the sand under the sun, close my eyes for a while, but I suspect then I will miss the sticky, sandy hands pulling me towards whatever project he has on the go and that little voice calling "Mummy!"

The afternoon fulfils its promise. We have lunch at the kitchen table, Sam reminding Sophie that phones are not allowed and to her credit a ready acceptance of this. She loves the pasties and exclaims over the meringues as though they are long-lost friends. Ben eats without protest and without thinking, it seems, so enraptured is he with his big sister.

Sophie clears up, without being asked (a raise of eyebrows from Sam) then we pick up our bags, which Sam got ready earlier, and Ben picks up his bucket and spade, and off we go to the bus stop by the swimming pool, catching one of the little buses that run a constant round tour of the town and which drops us off right at the bottom of the hill, near the cinema. From here it is just a few minutes' walk to the surfy beach – we let Sophie choose but already knew which it would be – which is gratifyingly quiet, given what a beautiful day it is.

I picture the M5 and the A30, and the hordes of holidaymakers heading down here, no doubt at a snail's pace – all those half-frustrated, half-excited people, just desperate to get here and for their holidays to begin. I imagine them bursting onto the scene later today – each car like a bubble popping and releasing its tightly-bound contents. Children, parents, grandparents, emerging from their cars, with bags and duvets, body boards and wetsuits, tumbling out. Legs and arms stretching. Eyes taking in the fresh, vivid sky and the bright, almost-white sand of the beaches; hearing focusing on the calls of the gulls, and the sound of the sea; noses and lungs filling with the clean, salty air. All the senses at once soothed and exhilarated as the relief of the end of a long journey washes in.

We lucky few, to be here already, set up at the far end, although it's a bit of a trek. We can claim a little space near the rocks where I first met Sophie, and enjoy a little sheltered sunshine without the sea breeze muscling in and breaking out goose pimples across our skin.

As soon as the bags are down, Ben is stripping off, exposing his little round belly with no inhibitions or care for how warm it is.

Sam laughs. "Isn't it a bit chilly for that, mate?"

"No."

"Ok! Come on then, let's get digging, shall we?"

While Sam and Ben get to work, Sophie and I carefully lay the blanket out and take a seat next to each other. I'm touched to find her leaning against me slightly. I am always aware of her age and her need for independence, and to be treated like a grown-up. It's the luxury of step-parenting, I suppose, that I can be a little more removed if I need to be, and I don't have all those memories and bonds from when she was a baby, or a toddler, or a little girl just starting school.

"How's life?" I ask her.

"Good."

"And is it good to be back here?"

"Yeah," she says with such enthusiasm it makes me smile. "This will always be home to me, you know, Alice."

"I'm glad. And your dad will be too, if you say that to him."

"I'll make sure I do. Or I'll try to. I don't think he likes me being in Devon," she says suddenly, her nose wrinkling in her concern; a little flashback to her younger days.

"Well, he misses you. Which is a good thing."

"I know. But I feel like I'm disappointing him, sometimes."

I look towards Sam and Ben, who are heading hand-in-hand towards the sea, their objective clear: collect seawater in the bucket, bring it back to the little hole they've just dug and feel disappointed when the water just soaks into the sand.

"Sophie," I turn to her. "You are not disappointing him. He misses you, of course. And maybe that's why you feel that way. It's hard for him, to tell you, and he thinks it will make you feel bad. For being in Devon. Which, I suppose, is what you're saying," I smile. "But he completely understands and he's happy that you're happy there. You are, aren't you?"

It's Sophie's turn to smile and just for a moment I feel like she's the older one here. "Yes, I'm happy. I would say if I wasn't. And I'm busy. I like going out, into Exeter. Seeing bands and that, which I wouldn't get the chance to do down here."

I think briefly of Janie and the things she is missing by being here. "But it's great you're doing that! God, Julie and I were out all the time when we were your age. I liked going to gigs, too." Oh, I sound so old. Like I'm trying to be cool.

But it seems Sophie is interested rather than as though she thinks I'm cringey. "Did you? Who did you see?"

"Oh, all sorts… The Levellers, the Cure, the Beautiful South, REM…"

"Wow! Did you? I'd love to have seen them. I really like old music, you know," she says earnestly.

Old music. Now that's depressing. I choose to ignore it. "Yes, and we had a great bunch of mates, like you do. We'd have parties, when our parents were away… I shouldn't be encouraging you to do that… and hang out at the park, or in town or eventually in the pubs that turned a kinder, blinder eye to their younger patrons' age…"

I feel like I'm turning wistful. Talking of a better time. Sophie is probably picturing it all in black and white.

"We don't really drink," Sophie says. "Well, some of my mates do, but to be honest it just makes them into idiots. We like to go into town, and we like hanging out at the beach, too. Some of them bring their guitars."

I smile. I like this idea, and I know it's not far from what Sam and Luke used to do, down here. "Sounds pretty perfect. I'd have loved that, growing up."

"Yeah, and Mum and Isaac let us use the yurts sometimes, if there's nobody staying.

"Wow, that must be pretty cool."

"It is. And Pete, he's the best guitarist, and lives on a farm – but he's really into animal rights. And he writes his own songs, and his parents let us stay at the farm sometimes, too, in this barn they've got."

"Sounds pretty amazing." I register the name 'Pete' in my mind, with interest.

"It's just… really good. And you know, there's loads going on with school, too, and I'm working on the set designs for the end-of-year play. Mum says it's OK as long as it doesn't interfere with my studying. And it's something I think I'd like to do, you know, as a career."

I sit back and listen happily to Sophie. She's so full of enthusiasm for life, and her friends, and it seems to me that she's in the right place, in Devon, even though I know how much Sam misses her. And I miss her, too. But neither of us would want her to lose all these great things she's found, or people. Particularly Pete, by the sound of it.

I see Sam now, heading back up the beach, pretending to be weighed down by the bucket of water; Ben giggling and dancing round his feet. Oh, it's hard, it's complicated, this life business. There is Sam with our son, and here I am with his daughter. I wish we could all be together more often but we have to accept that we can't. We have to make the most of now.

When Sam arrives back, I stand, and make a show of admiring how much water they've collected. Then Sam helps Ben push the bucket over so that the water tips into the hole, sits there momentarily, for a split second at most, before sinking into the sand and leaving a dark puddle shape where Ben's hoped-for pond should be.

"Come on, Ben," I say, hoping to head his abject disappointment off at the pass, "let's go and get some more water, shall we? Go and spend some time with your daughter," I say, turning to Sam, and he gives me a grateful smile, needing no further encouragement.

Ben and I wander barefoot down to the shoreline and I take in the feel of his little hand in mine. Such trust. I often think I need to take in every detail of times like these, for the days when he won't want to hold my hand anymore. A long way off yet, I hope, but I know to Sam it doesn't seem long since Sophie was this age; this size. And now look at her. It's hard to believe that this little boy trotting along happily at my side will be her age one day. Have his own group of mates. Perhaps be the one who plays the guitar and writes his own music and has admiring girls ("Or boys," I hear David's voice in my head.)

I smile down at my son and we scoop up the water in the bucket but as we turn and I see Sam and Sophie in relaxed conversation, leaning against the rock, I don't want to disturb them.

"Shall we paddle for a bit, Benny?"

"Yeah!" he says. "But what about the hole?"

"It will still be there." I gently, lightly, kick a little water at him, the droplets shining briefly in the light as they fly through the air.

"Hey!" He looks at his wet tummy, and shorts. Then he laughs. And he kicks back, really missing the water but nevertheless, I say, "Hey!" right back at him.

He sits suddenly, in the water, looking up at me and chuckling. My heart melts and I follow suit, although the water is cold and I'm still wearing my shorts and t-shirt, and I probably look like a bit of a weirdo. Who cares, though? I pull him to me and we sit, letting the waves come. They are inches deep and just about trickle over us but nevertheless they make Ben squeal. The sun is on our faces and shining across the sea and then Ben points and I see them, too. Dolphins! Glossy and dark against the light, throwing themselves up, over, and back into the sea.

"Dolphins, Ben!" I say, even though he pointed them out to me. "Aren't they amazing?"

But he's soon bored and is back up on his feet, kicking water at me. I want to watch the dolphins' progress but it seems that is not compatible with Ben's idea of fun and as I started this whole kicking-water-at-each-other thing, I can't really complain. I stand and growl, and chase after him, along the water's edge. There are other paddlers, and swimmers, some of whom smile at us. When I catch up with Ben, I swing him into the air, and pretend I'm going to throw him into the sea.

"No, no!" he squeals, laughing, and I bring him close to me, hold him tight, while my eyes just can't help looking out across the waves again but there is no longer any sign of the dolphins.

Eventually, we head back to Sam and Sophie, and the four of us spend a happy couple of hours chatting and playing in the sand until the day's warmth fades and it's time to admit defeat and head happily home. Ben falls asleep on the bus ride and Sam carries him all the way back to the house.

I can sense waves of contentment from Sam and it seeps into me, too. Sophie, though back on her phone, is still very much with us, and long may it continue.

9

"Are you sure you'll be OK with both of them?" Julie asks Sophie for the hundredth time. I have also asked this same question, a lot, and Sophie's answer is always the same.

"Yes, I'll be fine – and I'll have Amber with me. And I'll call if there's a problem. You just have to promise me to get them to sleep before you leave the house."

"OK. It's a deal. Wow. A night out. At the same time!" Julie says to me.

"It's certainly been a while."

"You guys go, and have a great time," Sophie smiles.

"Now, Sophie, if you were me, I'd be very suspicious of that smile," Julie says. "I know what I was like when I was your age, desperate for my mum to go out for the evening so I could get my mates round. Alice included."

"And we always behaved impeccably," I say with a smile.

"Yes, of course."

"Well, it's a good job I'm not you, isn't it?" Sophie grins cheekily. "Honestly, Amber will come round and we're going to watch a film and just have a bit of time together. I'm really looking forward to it."

"No boys?" Julie asks, only half joking.

"Of course not! We're baby-sitting, anyway. I promise you, we will be absolutely sensible and reliable and responsible and…"

"Aren't you boring?" Julie laughs and ducks out of Sophie's way.

This really is a rare treat, in all honesty. Luke is home,

and the four of us – Julie, Luke, Sam and I – are going to Paul and Shona's engagement party.

Sam has offered to drive so that we can enjoy a drink. Not that I intend to overdo it but I am looking forward to it. And I'm not much of one for getting dressed up but I know I need to make an effort for a party at Paul Winters'. And there's a small part of me that returns to that other party at his place, when he and I were seeing each other. We'd had a plan, that night, for me to stay, but sneakily, so that none of the gossips would know what was going on. It was thwarted in the end, and probably that was a good thing, though frustrating at the time.

When I see Sam freshly shaven, in a shirt and smart trousers, my heart melts a little. He also is not big on dressing up and he looks slightly shy when I step into the room to see him. "Do I look OK?" he asks gruffly.

"You look gorgeous," I say, kissing him.

He steps back slightly to look at me. "And so do you."

"Reckon we scrub up OK, eh?"

"I think we do."

"And we'd better start thinking about what we're going to wear for our wedding!" I can't help laughing as I say the words. We are actually getting married!

Sam, though, groans slightly. "That has got to be the worst part of it all. Do I have to wear a suit? I don't wear suits. Only to funerals."

"It doesn't have to be a suit," I say. "We should go shopping and see what we find."

"Shopping as well?" Sam grumbles. "I thought getting married was meant to be a good thing."

"It will be worth it," I say. "I promise."

Sam pulls me to him and kisses me slowly and carefully. My knees weaken a little and just for a moment I wish we were staying in this evening – just me and him.

But Luke and Julie are waiting for us, and our kids are both tucked up and snoring sweetly – Zinnia in her cot and Ben in his toddler bed, though in a way it would make more sense for it to be the other way round. Zinnia is still showing no signs of wanting to move anywhere independently while Ben is hard to keep contained.

Luke wolf-whistles as we enter the lounge.

"That for me, mate?" Sam asks.

"That's right, Sammy. I always did like you in a shirt. Alice, you look OK too." Luke grins, and hands me a gin & tonic. "One for the road."

"You say that at the end of the night, you idiot!" Julie laughs. "But yes, Sam and Alice, you both look gorgeous."

Julie, of course, looks stunning – wearing another amazing dress that she's found from hours of scouring charity shops. She takes Zinnia with her and they come back with books, toys, and nice little finds in the way of baby clothes and Julie clothes.

"You look acceptable," I say. We clink glasses and laugh.

"Haven't you gone yet?" Sophie calls from the kitchen, where she and Amber are rustling up a feast, giggling as they do so. I am so glad that Sophie's kept her friendships here – especially with Amber.

"Alright, alright. We'll be gone soon," Sam says. "Just remember to phone if there are any problems."

"I will, Dad! I've told you that a million times!" Sophie appears in the doorway.

"A million? I doubt it." Sam smiles and kisses his daughter. It's been good for them to have this week together. I hope that when she's gone back to Devon this good feeling stays with him. And I hope Sophie is just a bit better at keeping in touch.

"Thanks for doing this, Sophie." I smile. "And you, Amber!" I call through, then take a big gulp of my drink. "We had better get going," I say, looking at my watch.

"Yes, off you go!"

"Anyone would think you want to get rid of us, Soph," Luke says.

"As if."

And we're off, into the still-light evening. It feels good.

It's like old times, the four of us, crammed into the little red car. "For old times' sake," Julie had said, but I know it's partly her contrary nature – she wants to turn up at the house of millionaire Paul Winters in our battered old rust bucket. She is driving us there and Sam will be driving us back. I think she's looking forward to parking alongside the Teslas and BMWs and sporty little numbers that will be no doubt lining the parking area.

I think back to that previous party, when Paul had sent a car for me. Driven by, as it turned out, a friend of his – Jack. And I'd been mightily grateful for Jack and his wife Rachel at the party that night. I remember having felt quite lost, yet excited at the prospect of what I thought lay ahead later that evening. As it turned out, Paul was not to play the same part in my life that I had anticipated but has been arguably more important than a brief fling, which is all our fledgling relationship was destined to be. It was Paul who sold Amethi to Julie and me, though we didn't know it at the time. And he's helped us in countless ways with advice on the business, and helping us make contacts, followed by Shona helping us in countless ways with PR.

Back then, I think, as we turn into Paul's driveway, I could never have foreseen what has happened over the last few years. Not just the success of Amethi, but getting back together with Sam, and of course having Ben. I smile, and squeeze Sam's hand.

He turns to me, looking pleased. "What was that for?"

"Just because."

He puts his arm round me when we are out of the car, and Julie and Luke hold hands. The four of us approach the front door, which is opened for us by a smart, smiling young man. "May I take your names?" he asks politely, ticking us off on a list then ushering us in, where an equally smart young woman hands us glasses of sparkling wine.

"Julie! Alice!" I hear Shona's voice and turn. "And Sam and Luke, of course. I'm so glad you could all come. And nice to have a night away from the bairns, I bet?"

She looks absolutely beautiful, in a long plain burgundy dress, her hair tied loosely back and a string of diamonds around her neck.

"Hi Shona," I kiss her cheek, and hand her the gift bag. "This is from all of us."

"You shouldn't have. You didn't need to bring anything. But thank you." She takes the bag graciously and gracefully, and kisses the others in turn.

"You look amazing," Julie says.

"Well, so do you – and you, Alice."

"Congratulations, Shona," says Sam and she smiles at him. They have not met all that many times but I occasionally think there is the hint of them being co-conspirators. But that is probably all in my head; after all, Paul and I were never really together. But Sam's nose was put truly out of joint when Paul once came to my rescue when Mum was ill and still living in the Midlands, and I had to get to her. Then while all that nastiness was going on with Tony, a few years back, Julie and I both had our suspicions that it was Shona causing trouble. I shake these thoughts from my head. How up myself am I to think that Sam and Shona think this way at all?

"Hello, gorgeous!" A voice comes from behind me and Paul is turning me round, to kiss my suddenly blushing cheek. I shoot a quick glance at Sam, and he's looking at me but his expression is amused rather than hostile.

"Sam!" Paul has already turned to him, shaking his hand, and then Luke's, and then kissing Julie too. I will my red cheeks to tone it down a bit.

Paul slips his arm around Shona's waist and it's so obvious that they fit together so well. "I'm so pleased that you've been able to come. I remember what it's like when the kids are little. Hard to get a night out. Make sure you grab a drink as soon as you can. Mind you, don't overdo it, you'll regret it in the morning. Take it from the voice of experience!"

"So who's drawn the short straw?" Shona asks.

"That would be me," says Sam.

"Ach well, you'll be the one lording it over the others with a nice clear head in the morning!"

"That's what I'm thinking."

"You lot are still living together then?" Paul asks. "I have to say, I admire you for that. You must have a strong friendship."

"We're more like family, really... but less annoying," Julie grins.

"And we're looking for somewhere, aren't we, Sam?" Why do I feel the need to assert myself like this? I don't like the thought of Paul and Shona thinking Sam and I can't get our own place. Even though they're not judgemental types.

"Yeah, after the wedding," Sam says, smiling at me.

"You've set a date?" Shona asks, looking at Paul and smiling. They're so obviously in love and although I obviously would never want to be without Ben, there is a small part of me that envies them their absolute focus on each other.

"Yes," I say. "But it's just going to be a small wedding, really," I add, wondering suddenly if they would have expected to be invited.

"I don't blame you," says Paul. "You'll be much more relaxed if you just have your closest family and friends there, rather than the hundred-and-odd guests Melanie and I had. We'll probably go small, won't we, Shona?"

"Absolutely. The minimal fuss, I think."

I can only imagine how beautiful their wedding will be. And expensive.

"We haven't quite sorted the guest list yet, but we're getting married in June," I say excitedly, "so I suppose we'd better hurry up."

"Where are you doing it?" Shona asks.

Paul rolls his eyes. "Luke, Sam, I know this is horribly sexist, but do you fancy coming out onto the decking? We've got a pool table out there and I really fancy a game. And I think this lot might be onto the wedding talk. I'm not sure I've got it in me."

"This is your engagement party!" I blurt out. "What else should you be talking about?"

"Exactly… *engagement*," Paul grins. "I want to celebrate where we are right now, not start talking wedding details."

"You are so old school," Shona chides him. "And don't think you'll get out of the wedding planning, when it's time."

"Sure. Just let me enjoy tonight though, eh?"

Sam and Luke follow Paul outside, accepting the beers he casually grabs from a passing waiter's tray.

Shona rolls her eyes. "Tell me all, then," Shona says. "Actually, girls, hold that thought—" she disappears into the kitchen and comes out with a bottle of champagne, "– let's take this somewhere and have a proper drink and chat, shall we?"

"You had me at 'girls'," says Julie.

We find a place to sit, near the open doors, from where we can see the sea with the last vestiges of daylight in the sky above; ambers, pinks and reds, streaked smokily across the darkening sky.

"Ah, it feels like summer's finally on its way," sighs Shona. She sinks into the seat, her back to the rest of the room. "So tell me all, Alice. And Julie, I want to hear all about your wedding, too. I want ideas!"

I describe the Longhouse – and George, the thought of whom always makes me smile – and the woodland setting. The food options, and the outside bar that we can have if we'd like to. Sam and I have chosen 22nd June for our wedding date ("That's the date Paul and I met!" Shona exclaims with glowing eyes, adding slightly embarrassedly, "When did I become such a hopeless romantic?"). It's a rare time of summer quiet at Amethi, at the end of the solstice week. The solstice falls on a Thursday and the guests will be leaving on the morning of 21st June, which is also Ben's birthday. It's a lot to cram into a short space of time but there won't be anyone new checking in until the Saturday so we have nearly two full days. And I mean, who'd want to spend that precious time relaxing and recharging? No, why not cram a wedding into that gap instead? Much more sensible.

It's not far off and we have checked with all those we'd like to be there that they will be free. Our guest list so far comprises: Mum and Dad; Karen and Ron; Luke, Julie and Zinnia; Janie and Jonathan; Kate, Isaac, Jacob and of course Sophie; David, Martin, Esme and Tyler ("Do the

kids have to come?" Sam had groaned, only half-joking –
"I mean, Esme's fine, but can't Tyler go to school or
something?"); Christian and his new girlfriend, Sadie;
Luke's dad, Jim; Julie's mum, Cherry, and Julie's brother,
Lee. Bea and Bob will be in the States and can't make it,
unfortunately, but I thought that it might be asking a bit
much of them. That makes twenty-five people, including
me, Sam and Ben. It seems enough and I think it makes it
easier in the possible event of bad weather. If we do all end
up inside, there will be plenty of space.

To be honest, neither Sam nor I want anything huge.
We just want, after all this time, to get married. And also,
if we don't spend too much, we can still carry on the search
for our own home.

"It sounds perfect! And Julie," Shona turns to my friend,
"tell me all about your special day."

I sit back, happy to let Julie talk and relive her memories
of that beautiful day. I remember it so well myself and find
a couple of tears in my eyes at the thought of it. What a
time that was. Sam and I were not together and were not
really getting on. In fact, we had that horribly awkward
best-man-and-bridesmaid dance. I push that thought
away; think instead of the speech I made for Julie that day
and realise that I will probably have to do the same at my
own wedding – keep it even, and fair from the outset. If
Sam makes a speech then so should I.

Shona is quizzing Julie on all the minutiae. The food, the
drink, the decorations. I happily sit back and half listen,
while watching the game of pool taking place outside.
They've roped in Jack, by the looks of it, to play in teams
of two, and every now and then there is a burst of laughter.
It's nice to see them all getting on, and so nice to see Sam
relaxed and happy.

Beyond them, there is now no visual sign of the sea, but I can hear it, steady and reassuring. And below, I know, is the little secluded beach that Paul took me to on our very first date, when I had no idea that this house belonged to him.

I am having far too many thoughts of Paul, I realise, and I push them away, gladly replacing them with imaginings of Sam's and my wedding day. I can't believe it's really going to happen! And I know, we must be mad, wedging it into that small gap of otherwise free time but I feel like if we don't, it might never happen. Something else will come up: a house; another child (imagine that). *Carpe Diem*, as Dad would say.

And George seems to have it so well organised, I have every faith in him that it will all go according to plan. "Just think of it as a big party," he said. "Alice, you must be super-organised, doing the job you do. This is like a big family party, the only difference being you're also getting married."

"Oh yes, just that small detail," I'd replied.

"I'm pretty organised, too," Sam had mock-grumbled.

"Of course you are," I had soothed and George and I had shared a knowing look.

"Don't think I didn't see that."

In time, Shona of course has to go and socialise with other guests, but she kindly leaves the bottle with Julie and me, and we stay put, in our comfy seats, with a view of the rest of the room and the outside space, too.

It's so nice, just sitting with my friend, and for a while we don't talk at all; just relax, at complete ease with each other, and watch the goings on. The room is full of loud voices and laughter; suit jackets soon discarded and ties loosened, while women slip off uncomfortably high heels and dance to the acid jazz currently playing through Paul's incredibly expensive and apparently invisible sound system. Shona was right; it really does feel like summer's finally on its way.

"I can't wait till your wedding," Julie says. "I know, what they say about marriage, and that you and Sam are totally happy and secure with one another, but there is something magical about a wedding day. It's a chance to celebrate your luck at finding each other and, I don't know, there's something about the ritual. And all the people there, with you, wishing you happiness and love. It's quite something. I want that for you, Alice. And for Sam." Her eyes are shining.

"Julie, are you crying?"

"What? No! Maybe a little. I've got that thing you said about. After having Ben. Where everything seems so much more emotional, somehow. Everything means more."

"I know," I feel my own eyes filming over. "I know." I squeeze her hand. Then, sitting up straight for a better look, "Shit. I don't believe it."

"What?"

"It's her," I say. "It's Lydia."

This time, I think, she is not going to get away from me.

10

"Alice!" Lydia looks startled. Good. I've caught her on the back foot.

"Hello," I say, still not quite sure how to play this. "How are you?"

I shot straight up when I saw Lydia; onto my feet and across the room, leaving Julie slightly bemused on the comfy sofa.

"I'm fine," she says tentatively, having the grace to look slightly abashed. She looks so grown up – she *is* so grown up, I remind myself – with her long red hair now cut into a really smart, really short bob, shaved at the nape of her neck. And a black cocktail dress, and heels. It's a far cry from the slightly scatty, earnest girl I remember, working her hours as a waitress then settling down in the Sail Loft office to study in peace, away from her much-loved but very noisy twin brothers.

"Great. I heard you were back." I want her to tell me herself.

"Yes, I've… I had enough of life in London. I wanted to come back here. You know what that's like," she laughs slightly nervously.

"And you've got a job, have you?" I ask sweetly.

"I – yes. A job. Manager at the… at the Bay Hotel."

"I had heard that," I say, trying to hold onto the indignation I've been feeling but in honesty, faced with Lydia, who I've known since she was not much older than Sophie is now, it's hard to feel hostile. She's a lovely person. I know she is.

"Had you?" She seems to swallow. "It was very flattering to be asked."

"I'm sure, yeah."

"So what are you doing here?" she asks, gesturing to our surroundings.

"Paul's an old friend of mine," I say. "Shona, too. She does all the PR for Amethi. You know, the place Julie and I run."

"Oh, right," she says.

"What are *you* doing here?" I return the question.

"I'm with Felicity," she says. "My new boss. Her husband knows Paul."

"Really?" Is this a coincidence? I hope so. But weird that she'd asked Shona to do the PR for her, and they hadn't made the connection.

"Yeah, but he – Alan, Felicity's husband – couldn't come and she kind of insisted I come along instead. Said I might do some *networking*."

Her brow furrows as she says this word and I have a glimpse of the old Lydia.

"Ha! Yes, Paul's good at all that stuff," I say, finding my chilly veneer thawing. "He's helped me and Julie loads," I admit.

"And his wife? Fiancée," she corrects herself.

"Yeah, that's right." I decide there's no point pretending anymore. "And you know that because… *Felicity*… tried to pinch her off us."

"I wouldn't say that, exactly."

"Wouldn't you? She couldn't very well be doing our PR and the Bay's, could she? By the sound of it, we are offering *very* similar things." I raise an eyebrow, feeling emboldened by three quickly-drunk glasses of champagne.

"Yes, well, I suppose so," Lydia looks down.

"Come on, Lydia," I smile. "We might as well be honest. Yoga? Writing courses? Ring a bell, at all?"

"Honestly, Alice, I didn't really know you did all that. I only knew Felicity because I worked with her god-daughter in London and when Amy said about this new hotel, and where it was, it sounded like too good an opportunity to miss. I do like London, but really, I miss here. I miss home, and my family. I wanted to come back."

"I can understand that," I concede. "But whose idea was it, to run those kind of events?"

"It was all set before I was interviewed, I promise," says Lydia, her green eyes looking earnestly into mine. "And it did strike me as a bit odd but I thought it was a coincidence, really. I mean, these things are popular. Loads of places do yoga. And I remember Kate was going off to do a yoga retreat place, and that didn't bother you."

"No, but that's in Devon," I say. "Not on my doorstep."

"You're right."

"And the writing courses?"

"Oh, yeah, well Felicity's got all these contacts in the media, and she's going to run courses a bit like the ones you see in the Guardian. Different topics, like memoirs, and ghostwriting, and that kind of thing."

"OK," I say slowly, thinking that does sound a little bit different to our writing weeks at Amethi, which are more low-key, for writers to develop their style and work, and really just have the time they would never normally have, to write and write and write. "But why didn't you get in touch?"

"I was going to, I promise. But I suppose I did know you might be a bit pissed off."

"That's one way of putting it. But I'm pleased to see you, Lydia. I've missed you!"

Her face brightens. "Have you?"

"Of course."

"Even after what happened with Jon?"

"Of course," I say again. "These things happen. You were very young when you two were together. And you've always been very driven. It would have been too difficult for you to make that relationship work while you were so far away, and working so hard."

"But now I'm back here," she says.

"Yes," I take a sip of my drink. "You are." I smile. Then I think, *Hang on...* "But you know Jon's with somebody else now?"

"Yes, he did say."

"He said?"

"Yes, but he doesn't sound very happy."

"You've seen him?"

"No, not yet, but we've kept in touch, you know."

"Have you?"

"Yeah, just emails, mostly... you know, catching up with each other. Keeping up-to-date with things."

"So you know about Janie?" I hear alarm bells ringing.

"Yes, I do."

"And you know she's Sam's sister?"

"Oh, yeah, I think Jonathan mentioned that."

I feel my armour click back into place. I am so fond of this girl but it feels to me distinctly like she's presenting a threat. And not necessarily to my business – though I am not over that yet – but more to my (nearly) sister-in-law.

What has Jon been playing at? I want to know. I want to call him right away and find out. It feels all wrong. But I can't give anything away.

"Yeah, she's lovely," I say. "She and Jon met a couple of years ago and she lifted him straight out of a low patch.

They've lived together for quite a while now. They're very happy," I add meaningfully.

But it feels like Lydia isn't listening. I am not convinced that it will matter to her. Because I know Lydia, and her determination. It's got her to where she is now. She worked so hard, to get her A-Levels, and get to uni. She knew what she wanted to do and she bloody well did it, working all the hours she could at the Sail Loft to support herself and her studies, and to a certain extent her family. And back then, she wanted Jon, even though he was a pain at first, and unreliable. Somehow, he realised that he did want to be with her, and they were happy together for a while. But then she set her sights on something else: her career. Her relationship couldn't sit alongside that, and so it was goodbye to Jonathan. Now, she's back – and she's got an exciting new job, which I just know she is going to excel at; and it sounds to me like she might be focusing back in on Jon once more. Shit, I think, but I can't hate her for it. Far from it. She's got drive and ambition and those are not bad things. And besides, I can't help thinking, she reminds me so much of somebody else I know, who knows what she wants and goes for it. The person who persuaded me to move back to Cornwall.

"Well, good luck," I say, and I clink my glass weakly against Lydia's, turning slowly back to look at Julie.

11

"Tyler! Not up there! You're not old enough," David says despairingly.

We've brought the kids to a soft play place, the idea being that they can play while David and I drink coffee and chat. The reality is a series of disjointed conversations, three kids all going in different directions, and neglected coffee going cold on the table.

Still, it's so good to see him. It's been too long, which seems ridiculous given how close he and I live to each other – just a handful of miles along the estuary – but he works, Martin works, I work, Sam works; Tyler is now at school, and Esme at the nursery there, while Ben is at Goslings nursery and between us all it is very hard to be in the same place at the same time.

We had this 'play date' lined up four weeks ago, not long after Shona and Paul's party, but Tyler and Esme had both had a high temperature so we had rearranged for two weeks later. Then Ben had an upset tummy. Two weeks on again, we have finally managed to get together. It's a weekend off for me. Luke is back, and with Zinnia, while Julie is up at Amethi. Sam's currently doing god-knows-what; having a well-earned break, I hope (and not just because I'm hoping for the same tomorrow).

Tyler looks down on us from his lofty position, then laughs and throws himself forward, leaping onto a giant swinging ball and crashing against the bright soft sides of the play structure.

"I give up," says David, as Tyler whoops with joy and runs

back to clamber up and do the same thing all over again.

Meanwhile, Esme sweetly leads Ben up and down the slopes of the toddler area, and helps him onto the slide.

"She loves that," David says. "Makes a nice change for her to be the older one."

"Ben looks pretty happy too," I say. "Shall we risk it and actually sit down again or is that tempting fate?"

"Let's go for it!" David grins.

I pull a face at my lukewarm coffee and David insists on getting us fresh cups. "After all, it's not often we get to do this. Why ruin it with crap coffee?"

I sit back for a moment while he goes to the counter. Remind myself to roll my shoulders back, planting my feet firmly flat on the floor. Posture, and relaxation. I know how tense my muscles are. All the while, I keep an eye on the kids. Tyler appears to have buddied up with another boy, who looks a similar age to him, while Esme and Ben are still happily engaged and now taking it in turns on one of the little slides.

When David comes back, bearing two giant steaming mugs, I smile happily. "How is it possible to have such a nice time in such a nightmare of a place?"

"Ha! It's because the kids are occupied. And relatively safe. Save for the snot and the bogies in the ball pool, and the germs where some other kid's licked the slide…"

"Mmm. Thanks for that." I pretend to push my coffee aside.

"It's good for them! Builds up their immunity."

"Let's hope so."

"Anyway, quick, while we have the chance, tell me all about this wedding!"

"I will. I'd love to. Only, I'd kind of like to ask you about something else first."

"Alice, I've told you, I'm gay. And I'm married. I'm sorry, but you're just going to have to accept it."

"You wish!" I say. "Believe it or not, I wasn't going to talk about you."

"Ok. Weird. But go on."

"It's about Jonathan. And Janie. And… Lydia." It feels so good to be able to talk to David. I've been holding this knowledge to myself for weeks.

"Lydia? As in, Jonathan's ex, Lydia?"

"Yes, exactly."

"Is she back on the scene?"

I realise how long it is since we've had a proper chat and I fill him in on the situation with the Bay Hotel – to gratifyingly outraged gasps – and then Jon's and Janie's problems – ending with the conversation I'd had with Lydia at Paul and Shona's party. I didn't tell Julie what Lydia had said. And I haven't mentioned it to Jonathan yet, either. Or to anyone, in fact. I'm not sure what to make of it myself.

"So she's got a new job managing a hotel, and she's come back to Cornwall, and she wants to get back together with her old boyfriend," David sums up. "Sound like anyone we know?" He raises his eyebrows.

"Hey! That was different. For one thing, Sam was single. And I wasn't shafting a friend with a rival business, either. I'd been thinking she reminded me of Julie, not me!"

"I hope you haven't told Julie that."

"No, and I don't mean it as an insult, either. I've known Lydia for years. I do really care about her and I know how driven she is. The way I've described it, she sounds really selfish, and conniving – and I know that she is, in a way – but she has no particular reason to feel loyal to Janie. She's never met her."

"No, but I would say it's questionable, to say the least, to have the intention of breaking up an existing relationship."

"I can't say I disagree with that."

"Are you going to tell dishy Jonathan?"

"That's the other thing. I think he knows. Or at least he knows that she's back, if Lydia is to be believed. It sounds like they've never totally lost touch. Which is fine, I think, if Janie knows about it. Otherwise, there's something a bit underhand about it, wouldn't you say?"

"Yes… yes and no. It really depends on whether it's our Jonathan making the running, or at least participating equally – or if Lydia is contacting him and he's just politely replying but at the same time worried about telling Janie. Particularly if they're already having difficulties."

"You are very wise, my friend. I knew you were the right person to talk to."

At this moment, a very red-faced and out-of-breath Tyler appears, gulps down a plastic cup's worth of squash and dashes off again, without a word. I've kept an eye on Ben and Esme while we've been talking and they're just having the best time, now throwing plastic balls up above a blower to float into the air. Both laughing their heads off. It's very nice to see.

"I think you need to talk to Jonathan," David says.

"I think you're right."

"But?"

"But what do I say? Is it any of my business?"

"It is if he's talking to her about Amethi. If she's taking your ideas."

"I'm not sure if she is."

"No, but that is a legitimate reason to broach the subject."

"I guess."

"You know I'm right. I am very wise, remember?"

We have lunch at the play place, the kids tucking into fish fingers, chips and beans, while David and I eat paninis filled with melted cheese and startlingly hot tomatoes.

"You've got another half-hour," he tells Tyler sternly, "then we've got to get back home."

"And we're going to look at a house!" I say happily to Ben.

"There's something I want to talk to you about, actually, Alice," David says.

"Oh?"

"Yes, it's a little plan Martin and I have been concocting. We've talked about it ever since Bea went over to the States. We're going to take a trip over to see her and Bob."

"Oh wow, that sounds amazing."

"Yes, we're going for a year."

"A year? A… wow. That really does sound amazing."

"We just figured it's now or never, really. I can take a sabbatical from work and Martin can work from anywhere, really. It seems like the perfect time, before school gets too serious for the kids. Tyler can go to kindergarten and I think we'll just keep Esme home with us. She can start school next year, when we come back."

I try to take this all in. "You'll be going soon, then?"

"Yes, in the autumn. Late September, probably."

"Wow. Shit. What will I do without you for a year?"

"Alice, we haven't seen each other since February, I bet. A year will fly by, you'll see."

"I suppose so. And you'll be here for the wedding."

"Of course. As if we'd miss that."

"Well, in that case, I'm really happy for you. And excited! What a great thing to do."

"I know. And I get to see Bea and her ugly brute of a husband. We're renting near them and going to do some road trips while we're there; all six of us. I can't wait."

"I bet Bea can't, either."

"She does seem pretty excited. There was something else I wanted to talk to you about, though, to do with all this."

"Oh yeah?"

"Yeah, well our house is going to be empty and will need looking after. We wondered if you and Sam would like it while we're away? We'd need to charge rent of course," he adds, keen to get that in, "but it would be very reasonable. We'd be happier to know it's being lived in by people that we know."

"Oh wow," I say again. "I'm… that's lovely of you. I don't know. We're looking at trying to buy a place…"

"I know, we just thought this would give you more time to save up."

"Well, that's true, I, erm…"

"You don't need to say right now. You need to talk to Sam of course, anyway."

"Of course. Thank you, David, that's lovely of you."

"No pressure, Alice, OK? We'll be able to find somebody else."

"Yes, thank you, David."

It is a lovely house; really lovely, in fact, with its views of the estuary and nestled into the woods at the edge of the little village. I think of David and Martin's wedding reception, at the village hall there, and how friendly all their neighbours were.

There is no way we could ever afford a house like theirs, I know, but at the same time I really think we need our own place, now. Mine and Sam's, and Sophie's and Ben's. Still, it's something to think about.

12

Ben, predictably, falls asleep on the way to the house viewing. Sam gently unstraps him from his seat and lifts him onto his shoulder, where he grumbles when Sam greets the estate agent.

"Sam? Alice? I'm Roger." He shakes our hands. "And this must be Ben!" The man's on the charm offensive, already. "How are you, buddy?"

Ben is giving nothing away.

"He's just woken up," I explain apologetically. "This place looks nice," I offer hopefully. And it does. It is perfectly nice. It's a four-bed detached house on the newish estate at the opposite edge of town to Julie and Luke's house. It's a fifteen-minute walk down the steep hill into town. Probably double that to get back up here. And there is no view, of course, of the sea. This is only to be expected and, really, that is a luxury that neither Sam nor I expect to have. But I'll miss it. We've been spoiled, so far.

We walk behind Roger up the short, paved path to the front door. It's neat, and tidy, as are the houses either side. They have shiny cars parked on their driveways and there is the distinctive sound of a trampoline being used in one of the neighbouring gardens. Happy children's voices.

Inside, the house is clean and tidy and decorated ever so neutrally, with magnolia paint on every wall and cream-coloured carpets. The kitchen is large and modern, with space for a dining table, and there is a conservatory pinned onto the back of the house.

"The present owners added this. I think they used it as a playroom when their kids were little," Roger adds, and I don't know if that's true or not but it's certainly an attractive idea, rather than having the lounge a permanent mecca for Ben's toys.

Upstairs, the master bedroom has a small en suite, and the three smaller bedrooms have built-in wardrobes. It is neat, efficient and modern, and really a very nice house. I suppose it's just that it's so different to the places we've lived before. I look at Sam to try and work out what he's thinking. Ben is sucking his thumb sleepily, head against Sam's shoulder.

"I'll let you guys have a wander round yourselves," Roger says. "I'll just be outside."

"Thank you," says Sam.

"So, what do you think?" I ask, when Roger's safely out of the way.

"I like it," says Sam.

"Do you?" I ask brightly. This is a positive. He's been very negative about the other places we've seen to date. Which haven't, in honesty, been all that different from this one.

"Yeah," he says. "It's nice being on the edge of the development. Over the road it's just trees, isn't it? So we're not overlooked by anyone from the front."

He's talking like it's already ours. And it's improving my feelings for the place. I really think that, despite having lived in that dream house right in town, I could be happy here, as long as Sam is – and Ben and Sophie, too, of course, but I think they would be happy in most places. And that's not to say that it's all about Sam, but really, I would just like a nice family home, where we can stop and stay for as long as we want. A place which is ours (and the mortgage lender's, of course, but we'll ignore that for now).

I peer out of the front bedroom window. Roger is leaning on his car, intent on a phone conversation. Sam is right;

across the road is a long line of trees. Behind them, a busyish road, but on the other side of the road lie fields and farms and, eventually, the moors.

It would be five or ten minutes' drive from here to Amethi, or twenty minutes by bike (let's think big here, Alice). A similar amount of time to walk to Ben's nursery. Sam's office is out of town anyway, over in Penzance, and from here he'd easily be out on the road whenever he needs to. This place really is starting to grow on me.

"What do you think, Ben?" I ask.

Ben just looks at me. His blue eyes, so like his dad's, tell me he has no idea what I'm talking about.

"Do you like this house?"

"Yeah!" he says.

"That's settled it, then," Sam smiles at me. He puts Ben down and puts an arm around me. "What do you think, Alice? Do you like it?"

"Honestly… it's lovely. It's in great condition, and it feels really quiet up here."

"But…?"

"No, no buts, not really. I know we could never afford what Julie and Luke have, or somewhere in town. This place is lovely and it has loads of space. And a garden for Meg, and for Ben."

"And for us! It's a bit plain at the moment but I reckon we could Ground Force it. Make it a bit more private."

As he speaks, a feeling grows within me, of hope and happiness. I could see us living here. Me, Sam and Ben, and Sophie whenever she's in town. And who knows, maybe we'll fill that fourth bedroom one day…

I move into one of the back bedrooms and look down at the garden, which I have not yet really taken in. I can see the kids on the neighbours' trampoline. Two little girls, bouncing for all they're worth. I smile, wondering if they're sisters or friends. A man is hanging up washing on a rotary drier. He says something to the girls and I hear their squeals but I can't hear his words so I guess we're pretty well insulated and the double glazing's doing its job.

Sam is right, that our garden – am I really calling it ours already? – is a bit plain, and overlooked by our neighbours as much as theirs is by us, but we could definitely do something about that. Beyond the back fence stand more houses. The estate. Then beyond them is the town, and the harbour; the beaches and the sea. We will not be quite so close to them and I will miss that, but there are buses. And we have a car. And bikes. And feet. Imagine how fit I could get walking up and down the hill to town.

Ben is at my feet, grasping my leg, asking to be picked up. I oblige and show him the garden. "Do you like it, Benny?"

"Trampoline!" he says, pointing at the neighbours'.

"Yes, but that's in a different garden. But maybe we could get one of those," I say.

"Steady on!" laughs Sam. Then, "Maybe we could."

We walk around the house together, looking carefully in every room. It is a strange feeling, looking round somebody else's home. The owners have cleared off for the day, having first cleaned and tidied the place so it's almost immaculate, but their personal items are everywhere. On the mantelpiece, a proud photo of a girl in graduating robe and mortarboard, grasping a scroll. On the walls, printed canvases, of a girl and a boy, on bikes and on scooters. A school photo, of the two children a little bit older.

In the study, there are old photos, in sepia and black-and-white, of young men and women from days long gone. Smiling faces on a day trip to the beach. A young man stands proudly at the top of a hill, feet encased in sturdy boots, one atop a rock, claiming the summit as his own. The pictures are faded and some are wrinkled, but lovingly placed in frames and hung upon the walls. I wonder who these people are or, more correctly, were. I love to think that each one of these people had their own story; their loves and losses, successes and disappointments. What they would make of the world as it is today, who knows? Sophie on her phone all the time. Me and Julie, with our own business. Luke and Sam, hands-on dads. Maybe I do these people in the pictures a disservice to think they would be shocked by any of this. But it feels like things have changed so much. I suppose they always will.

This house has a nice feel to it. Peaceful, warm and calm.

"I like it here," I say to Ben.

"Me, too," Sam says, putting his arms around us both. "Me, too."

We thank Roger and tell him we'll be in touch, then we head home – or to Luke and Julie's home – to find Luke and Zinnia asleep on the settee, Mr Tumble on the TV.

"Tumble!" Ben says excitedly and he settles down on a chair, pulling the cushion over his knees.

"Should we wake them?" Sam gestures to Luke and Zinnia but our friend is already stirring.

"When did you get back?" he asks sleepily.

"Only just. You enjoying Mr Tumble, then?" asks Sam.

"Oh yeah, this one's been gripping. As you can see, Zin's totally into it."

Against all odds, she's still asleep. Determinedly so.

"How was the house?" Luke sits up, easing Zinnia gently onto the cushions.

"It was nice," I say, smiling at Sam. I'm aware I keep using the word 'nice' and Julie's and my English teacher,

Mr Hubbard, would have my guts for garters if he could hear me.

"Just nice?" Luke smiles.

"No, more than that." It isn't exciting, in the way that the old house is – tucked away on one of the central streets heading towards the harbour, steeped in history and part of the fabric of the town. And it isn't modern and sleek like Luke and Julie's place, with its 'clean lines' and far-reaching views towards the sea. But it is a lovely place. And I could imagine us living there; far more than any other place we have seen. "I really liked it."

"I did, too."

"Well then, that is exciting. And calls for a beer, wouldn't you say?"

"You've only just woken up!"

"That was a power nap. And I only mean one beer. It is Saturday, after all."

We leave Ben and Zinnia in the lounge and go into the kitchen, where Luke pulls three bottles from the fridge and we all sit at the table.

"How was David?" Luke asks, efficiently clipping the tops off the beers.

"Oh, great," I say. "Actually, Sam, I forgot to tell you, he and Martin are going abroad for a year. To the States."

"And leaving the kids?"

"No, I'm pretty sure they'll be taking them. They're going to rent a place near Bea and Bob. And they did ask if we wanted to live in their place while they're gone."

"Really? That's quite a place," says Luke.

"Yeah…" I say reluctantly. "It is." I look at Sam to see what he makes of the idea.

"I don't know," he says. "I think I've had enough of borrowing other people's places. No offence, mate," he says to Luke. "You know how much we appreciate you and Julie letting us stay here."

"None taken. I totally get it. You need your own place. But you're welcome to be here as long as you want."

"Thank you, Luke," I say, pleased Sam said what he did. I don't want to influence him in any way. He's been fed up and I want to make that better. I hope that having our own place will contribute to that. I think of David and Martin's home wistfully. If we could afford a place like that, it would be amazing, but I really agree with Sam. It's time we stopped relying on other people. It feels like we'll be striding out ourselves. Together. And getting married, too! This might just turn out to be the best year ever.

13

On Monday morning, Sam kisses me goodbye, and takes Ben with him so that he can drop him at nursery on his way to work. We have a plan! Sam is going to phone Roger first thing this morning and make an offer on the house. I can't believe it, and have started to feel really excited, my feelings about the place having progressed from 'nice'.

"It's lovely," I told Mum and Dad yesterday when I dropped in to see them. "I mean, it's a bit out of town, but not too far, really. And a short walk to school, when that day comes."

"Imagine that," Mum said wistfully, looking out at Ben who was pushing gravel out of the edge of the patio. The sky was a vast sheet of blue and the air beginning to take on a warmth of its own, seemingly independent of the sun. Those red flowers at the steps of the Sail Loft are starting to bloom, and although the place looks very different now to when I worked there, it all felt so familiar. Like home.

"I can't think about it!" I said. "He's growing up too fast."

"Time for another?" Dad said.

"Phil! You can't say that. Alice and Sam might not want another. Or be able to have one," she said sternly. I thought of Julie, and of Mum losing a baby, when I was little. I know Mum was thinking the same.

"It's OK, Mum. I feel like what will be, will be. I wouldn't say no to another, though. One day."

"You did OK, as an only child," she said.

"I did. Anyway, I have so much to think about now. The wedding. The house… if they accept our offer, of course."

"Oh, I hope so. I do think it would do you good to have your own place, you know. You and Sam."

"And it would make a big difference to Sophie, too, I think. Even if she doesn't say anything, it's not ideal for her, having to use the guest room when she comes to visit."

"She'll be wanting some privacy, I should think, as well," Mum said. "Young girls do. You know that."

"And young boys!" Dad protested.

"Yes, of course."

"So, anyway," I said, "be thinking of us tomorrow and send good vibes, or thoughts, or prayers, our way, please."

"We most certainly will."

To Julie, when she had come back from work on Saturday, I'd said, "I'm starting to love it. But I can't get too excited. We haven't even made an offer on it yet."

"No, well, you're right. But it sounds like you've found the right place. But if it doesn't work out, you know you can stay here as long as you like."

"I know. Thank you, Julie."

"It's a pleasure. Honestly, I love having you around. To be honest, I'm getting fed up of Luke being away so much. I think we need to make some changes, too."

"To change, then," I said, holding up my beer bottle.

"How many of them have you had?" she asked.

"Oh, just two. Or three, maybe," I said.

"And the boys?"

"Yep. Them, too."

Luke and Sam had taken Meg out for a walk. I suspect a pub may also have been involved. So tea, bath and bed for the kids was very much up to me and Julie but I didn't mind. I was suddenly full of enthusiasm and optimism.

I insisted Julie have a relaxing bath, with a beer, while I

switched to tea and Responsible Mummy, making soup and toast for both Zinnia and Ben, and sitting between them both, right in the line of fire, while they took intermittent mouthfuls between dropping toast on the floor and firing spoonfuls of soup at the table or each other.

"You're going to miss this," I murmured, despite the mess. "And I will, too."

In the evening, once the kids were in bed and Sam and Luke back from their lengthy 'walk', a tired Meg drinking greedily from her bowl then settling happily into her basket, the four of us ordered an Indian takeaway and cracked open a bottle of wine, then another.

The evening was light and airy and the windows open, letting the light breeze in, to drift across our faces and ripple the takeaway menu left open on the windowsill.

"It's been lovely having you here," Julie said. "All of you."

"We haven't gone yet," Sam laughed.

"We're talking like we're definitely getting that house," I said. "We haven't even put in an offer yet. And if we do, it might be rejected."

But somehow, it felt like we knew, all of us. Some things are just meant to be.

I only had one glass of wine, but the others drank much more, and the conversation turned to Luke's work, and trips abroad.

"It's time for change," he said, almost echoing Julie's words from earlier.

"To do what?" I asked.

"To be here. At home. I miss my girls too much."

"You soft bugger," Julie said but I could tell she was pleased.

"I've got Jack in London, now, who is at least as good as me at my job. Probably better, if I'm honest. I'm tempted to hand over the operational side of things to him. Then I won't have to be over there so often – barely at all, if I'm lucky."

"And what about India?" This is Luke's passion, I know. The work he started with the charity he and Julie both became involved in – working with kids who had been employed in factories, missing their education and any chances and opportunities that should have been theirs.

"I don't know," he sighed. "That, I still need to work out. But even if I just cut out the trips to London, that means I'll be home much more. And I do love India – and keeping that link for Zinnia. It's her roots, isn't it?"

"Yep," said Julie. "And that's important, somehow, even though I don't suppose she'll remember it."

"We'll work it out," Luke smiled at Julie, and I saw the same look I'd seen so many years ago when as an eighteen-year-old he was besotted by my friend. It was another ten years on that she realised she felt the same about him.

I couldn't help smiling at Sam, as I sat back in my seat, completely full – not just of curry but of love and warmth for the three people I was sitting with, and those two smaller people curled up safely in their beds not far away.

Now, though, I am facing a slightly less pleasant situation – or at least one with the potential to be so. I need to speak to Jonathan.

"Morning, Alice!" he says, as I push open the door to the kitchen.

"Hi, Jon, how was the weekend?"

"Oh, good, thanks. Busy. Did Julie tell you the Connors wanted a full Sunday roast yesterday? It was so hot in the kitchen! I need to get my summer whites out."

"Well done, Jon, that's going above and beyond."

"Ah, it's fine, you know. And I still got to go to the beach after."

"Did Janie go?"

"No," he looks glum. "She said she was going to see her mum."

"Oh, that's right – Sam popped over too, and said he'd seen her. So you went to the beach on your own?"

"Yes," he snaps. "Sorry, it's just you sound like Janie."

"Do I?"

"Yeah, I don't know what's got into her lately."

"Things not any better, then?"

"Not really."

And I might be about to make things worse, I think.

"Jon?" I begin.

"Yeah?" He has his back to me, dispensing fresh coffee into two cups.

"Do you know Lydia's back?"

I see his shoulders tense slightly. I wonder if he's setting his expression, before he turns around. Or deciding what to say.

When he does look at me, he is giving nothing away. "I... yeah..." he admits.

At least he's being honest. If he'd said no, I don't know what I would have done.

"How do you know?" he asks, but doesn't wait for an answer. "Don't tell me... the Bay?"

"Yes, well that's part of it. Listen, have you got a couple of minutes?"

"Sure." He looks worried.

"Come on, let's sit outside."

"OK."

He follows me out and we sit where we did the other week, looking out across the meadow, which has already begun to develop more colours amongst the green, green leaves and grasses. Tiny flower heads burst into life in purples, whites and oranges. Oxeye daisies flutter their eyelashes at us. *He loves me, he loves me not.* I'm so glad I don't think that way about Sam anymore. I wonder if it's how Janie feels about Jon, though.

"I saw her," I say. "More than once, in fact."

First, I tell him about seeing Lydia in town, when she didn't see me. Then I tell him about seeing her at Paul and Shona's party. I leave out the bit about Julie phoning the Bay. I don't think it shows us in a very good light.

"So she said you'd been in touch," I say gently.

"Well, we have, in a way…"

"Like you've never lost touch with each other?"

"Well no, we haven't," he says defensively, "but that's allowed isn't it?"

"Of course!" I say quickly. "But does Janie know?"

"Erm… no, I don't suppose she does," he says sheepishly. "But honestly, Alice, there is nothing *to* know. Lydia is way in the past for me, and I promise it's her that gets in touch with me."

I feel uncomfortable. "You don't have to promise me anything, Jon. And I'm sorry because I'm not sure this is any of my business. Really, my main concern was about this new hotel of hers, and how it seems to have a lot of similarities to what we do at Amethi."

"What, and you think I've been feeding her information?" he scoffs, looking annoyed.

"No, no, of course not…" Oh, where am I going with this? "No, I just. It surprised me when she said you were in touch. And I am, you know, Janie's sister-in-law, nearly. And I know you two haven't been altogether happy lately."

"Oh what, and you think I'm cheating on her with my ex?"

"No, and I didn't say that. But…" I think quickly. Should I say this, or not? I decide I should. "But I would say Lydia might still be interested in you."

"Don't say that, Alice."

"It's true. She pretty much told me, though not in so many words."

"Alice, it was ages ago, me and Lydia. We were different people then. And I love Janie."

"Good."

"And I promise it's always Lydia who instigates any contact. But I am really sorry I didn't tell you about her coming back, and managing the Bay. I should have, but, well, I was worried it would look like there was something between us. And judging by this conversation, I was right."

"Oh, I'm sorry, Jon. I really feel shit talking to you about this and I don't for a minute think you'd cheat on Janie. Of course I don't. But you need to watch out for Lydia."

"What? Because I'm a feeble man who won't be able to control himself?" His eyes look dark and angry and I feel lost in what I'm trying to say, and where I can go from here. And I feel awful for saying anything at all. Bea flashes into my mind; when she tried to warn me off Paul, all those years ago. I was so annoyed at her for sticking her nose in and now it seems I'm doing the same to Jon.

"I mean it, Alice, she was a long time ago. I'm not interested."

"I know. I believe you. I'm sorry, Jon. I really am."

"And yeah, things aren't great between me and Janie right now but that's got nothing to do with Lydia."

"Lydia?" Both Jon and I had heard the crunch of gravel at the same time, and then Janie's voice. Small, and quiet in the open air. "What about Lydia?"

"Oh god," Jonathan says, and as Janie turns and flees

back to their house, he stands up and follows her, leaving me sitting at the table with two half-drunk cups of coffee, a blackbird keeping a knowing eye on me from the fence. I'm sure it's telling me something. Something I already know.

You should have kept your mouth shut.

14

"He's going to call back!" Sam says, when I answer the phone.

All has been quiet at Amethi this last hour or so, save for the sounds of some of our guests traipsing across the gravel in the direction of the car park. It's not a very busy week, with just three of the houses full. It means Jonathan's not too busy and I hope very much that he and Janie will have the chance to sort things out.

What can I do? I've been wondering. I can't very well go over there and explain my part to Janie. Anything I say will be like adding fuel to the fire. I've been staying out of the way, up in the office, and having a WhatsApp chat with Lizzie about the forthcoming solstice week. It's just over two weeks away now... which means so is the wedding! But now I've blown everything, or at least it feels that way.

With so much on my mind, when Sam rings it takes me a moment to realise what he's referring to. He means Roger, of course. About our offer on the house. "Oh, really?" I ask, summoning as much brightness to my voice as I can.

"Yeah!" Followed immediately by a suspicious, "What's wrong?" There is no fooling this man.

"It's... oh god, I've done something really stupid..." I end up pouring it all out, from seeing Lydia at Paul and Shona's – what had she said then? *But now I'm back here –* up to this morning, to speaking to Jon, and his anger and denial, and also Janie's turning up at exactly the wrong moment, and how I haven't seen either of them since.

"Bloody hell, Alice, and you didn't think about telling me any of this?" The joyful tone from Sam's voice is all but gone now. "My sister's boyfriend might have been cheating on her, and you didn't think it was worth telling me?"

"He hasn't been cheating on her, Sam."

"Oh really? You know that for a fact, do you? I mean, this is Jonathan we're talking about. The same Jonathan you used to criticise for his bad attitude towards women, and his untrustworthiness."

"Well, yes, but… that was a long time ago."

"A leopard doesn't change its spots, Alice."

"Oh come on, Sam." I'm annoyed now, and defensive on Jonathan's behalf. "He was in his early twenties then. And he changed when…" I let the sentence tail off but Sam finished it for me.

"When he got together with Lydia?"

"Yes. But that doesn't mean he wants to be with her now. It just means he grew up."

"Really?"

"Yes. Really."

"OK, nice to know where you stand."

"Sam, you're being ridiculous!" I say, angry and frustrated tears springing to my eyes. Just when I thought we'd cracked his unhappiness; just when I was beginning to relax a little again and look forward to our wedding. And this isn't even our argument!

I should have told him, though, about Lydia. That night, after the party. But he'd seemed so happy, and I hadn't wanted to ruin it.

We'd returned home, Sam driving, at about half-eleven.

"Wonder what the girls are up to?" Julie had said.

"I imagine they're just watching a film, or playing on

their phones or something," I said.

"So disappointing," she shook her head in mock-disappointment. "Whatever happened to drunken teenage shenanigans?"

"I think what happened," Sam said, "is that this generation took one look at our generation, and the way we still can't draw the line when it comes to drink, and thought, no thanks."

"Plus," Luke interjected, "might I remind you that they are responsible for two very small human beings?"

"Well, yeah, but at least they could have some boys round or something."

"Julie!" I laughed. "Most people would be horrified at the thought of their babysitter inviting their boyfriend round! You must be the only person I know who's actually disappointed that they haven't."

"What can I say? I'm wild at heart."

"You're just not ready to be a grown-up," Luke teased and I turned round, slightly, in time to see him pull her to him, and kiss the top of her head.

"The only problem is, you're a mummy now, Julie. You can't be the irresponsible one anymore."

"I don't see why not. Somebody's got to be and Sam and Kate have obviously failed to pass that mantle on to Sophie."

We'd laughed and I'd looked across to Sam, smiling as he drove us home. I'd felt very content and relaxed and, yes, not willing to rock the boat. Lydia could wait, I'd thought. I would find the right moment to tell him. But I didn't, because we were having a nice weekend. And Sophie was going back to Devon, which I knew would make him feel sad – and it did but I was relieved that it didn't seem to make him feel too awful. After he'd taken her to the station, he came back home looking a little forlorn but he took Ben into the garden, where they planted out some of the plants we've grown from seed, and that seemed to cheer him up. I was relieved.

When will I ever learn, that not saying something is almost guaranteed to make a situation worse?

You should just be honest, I chide myself now. *You know that.*

There is a beep on the line now. A rustling at Sam's end.

"It's Janie," he sighs. "I'd better take this. But I'm meant to be working," he grumbles.

Well you phoned me, I think, but I do know that there are some things which are genuinely better left unsaid. Instead, I say, "OK. Well, let me know when you hear back from Roger."

"Will do."

And that's that. The call ends and I'm left holding a silent phone to my ear. I put it down and turn to my computer. I'll email all the solstice yoga guests with their welcome instructions. Then I can sort out all the filing on my computer, and the paperwork in the in-tray, and... I am sure I can find plenty to do to keep me busy up here, tucked away from the problems out there. Hopefully Sam will call back at some point, too – maybe even with good news from Roger. But it feels like that will be tainted now, with this stupid situation leaving a bad taste in my mouth.

Coming back to Cornwall; managing a rival business; threatening the happiness of Jon and Janie, and causing problems for me and Sam... I should hate Lydia, but despite it all, I can't help remembering that young woman who came to work at the Sail Loft. I had a sisterly, almost maternal, affection for her then and I still do now. I might have to toughen up, though.

In the end, Sam doesn't call back and I can only assume he is still waiting to hear from Roger, and still annoyed with me.

Somebody who does call is George. "Hi, Alice! How are you this fine day?"

"Oh hi, George." I was quickly getting myself together, having been disappointed that it wasn't Sam. "I'm fine, thank you. Busy as ever! How are you?"

"Oh, just fantastic!" he exclaimed. "I thought you'd like to hear how the wedding went this weekend... you know, our trial run in preparation for yours!" He laughs.

"Sure," I can't help smiling. He is just unstoppably enthusiastic. "I'm guessing it went well?"

"Oh, it did. It was beautiful. The bride was beautiful, the weather was beautiful, the Longhouse was beautiful, if I may say so myself. Keep an eye on the website, because Imogen's updating it now, with pictures. I was going to ask, actually, whether you and Sam would be happy for us to do the same with photos from your big day? Which is not too far off now!" he adds, as if I need reminding.

"Oh, er, I don't mind, at all, but I'd better check with Sam." But probably not today, as I suspect I'd just get a resounding no.

"Great. Thanks, Alice. And is now a good time to run through everything? Numbers, menus, special diets, and all that...?"

"OK," I say, "let's do it."

It cheers me up, running through all these details with George, and I must admit I enjoy having somebody look after me for a change – rather than me looking after the requirements of our guests at Amethi. It feels very nice.

"So it's salmon for the non-veggies and warm goat's cheese, pear and walnut salad for the veggies among you?"

"Yes, I think so – do you think that's enough?" I have a moment of doubt, that offering a salad as a main course at a wedding isn't really suitable.

"I'm sure it is," George soothes. "Remember, we've got all the freshly-baked breads and oils, and antipasti on each table, too. And, fingers crossed, it's going to be hot. People won't want a big pie and mash, or anything stodgy. I'd say salad is perfect."

"Thank you, George," I say, wishing Sam was part of this conversation, too. I want us both to be equal in this, our wedding day, as much as in our married life. But I know he won't be too worried about having missed this.

"For the kids, we've got fish fingers, potato waffles, beans… and some breadsticks, carrot sticks and houmous for snacks. Is that right?"

"Perfect."

"Crème brulee, chocolate brownie, and Lowe Hill Farm ice cream for dessert?"

"Lovely."

I start scribbling this all down, even though I know it, but it might give me a reason to call Sam.

"And can we just confirm your guest list, the timings, and so on?"

"Of course."

By the time I have finished talking to George – or, more accurately, he has finished talking to me; after we've gone through the wedding plan he proceeds to tell me about Imogen's parents' home renovations – I feel slightly better. I will call Sam, I decide. I'm getting married to the man in two weeks' time, for god's sake. I should smooth out the angst between us, and I would also like to know if Janie's OK.

I click on 'recent calls' and Sam's smiling face appears on my screen. I press it and hear the call go through. It rings out and goes to voicemail. "Hi, Sam. It's me. I hope you're OK, and I hope Janie was OK, too. Give me a call when you can. I've just got off the phone to George, about our wedding day. I can't wait!" The brightness in my voice is not all put on. That phone call genuinely has breathed some excitement back into me. "We've gone through all the details and I wanted to run them past you, too. You know, make sure you're happy with them. I was wondering if you'd heard from Roger, as well. Anyway, I know you're probably busy at work so just give me a call when you can..." *Shut up now, Alice*, I tell myself. This is far too long-winded and babbling. "OK. Bye."

I hang up and feel my cheeks grow warm, even though there is nobody here to have witnessed my idiotic voicemail.

I can hear the sound of pots and pans in the kitchen so Jonathan must be getting to work down there. I will leave him to it for now, though. I don't know what I can say to who at the moment so it's probably best I don't say anything at all.

I turn back to my computer and open up my email inbox. Only 347 emails to sort through. Still, it will keep me busy till Sam calls back.

15

Only, he doesn't call back. All I get is his answerphone message when I try to ring him and, eventually, a text.

Going to see Janie after work. She's upset, understandably. Don't know what time I'll be back.

No kiss. Nothing. How I hate texts sometimes – and also how childish is Sam that he can't even speak to me directly, or at least make his message a little less hostile?

I hate thinking like this about him. He's the man I love. And in so many ways he's always been so together and grown-up; even when we first met, I remember my humiliation when I thought he'd be impressed by my drunken foray into the sea but instead it had earned me a lecture on respecting the water and understanding the risks. Then of course, a little further down the line, he got together with Kate and they discovered she was pregnant by somebody else. Instead of cutting and running, he stayed with her. Even when he and Kate split up, he remained steady and reliable. He always has been, and always will be, Sophie's dad.

This is why it rankles so much, I think, that he is behaving this way now. And that these last few months he has been... grumpy. It's out of character, really, and hard to live with. Like a dark cloud hovering over us. But I know, of course I do, that at the root of it is his love for Sophie, and how much he misses her. He feels pushed out of her life now, which I think he has to be; it's what teenagers do, to start to feel their own way into the world. I don't suppose it is ever easy but I guess it's even less so when you're miles apart.

And now he's leaping to Janie's defence, though he knows very little about what is going on. Only as much as I know – that she and Jon have been having problems for a while and that Lydia is back and seems to have Jon in her sights.

The feeling gnaws away at me; that Sam is unhappy and angry at me, and it feels very unfair. And we're meant to be getting married in two weeks!

I decide to stop hiding in my office. I will pop my head round the kitchen door to say hi to Jon but I won't stop to chat. For one thing, I'm desperate for a wee. For another, I just don't want to get dragged into this situation any further. Only, when I do stick my head round the kitchen door it's Julie, not Jonathan, that I see.

"Hello!" I say, surprised.

"Oh hi! Where have you been?"

"I was in the office, of course."

"Were you? The door was shut and it was so quiet I assumed you must have been out on site somewhere."

"Ah. No. I was just keeping my head down."

"Oh?"

"Yeah. Bit of a nightmare. Nothing major but it's all gone a bit to shit today. Where's Jon, anyway?"

"He called me and asked if I could fill in. Said he had some kind of family emergency but nothing to worry about – which doesn't make a lot of sense, to be honest."

"No. OK. Have you got time for a coffee?"

"Yeah, in a few minutes. I'll just get these in the oven." She gestures to two large roasting trays filled with clean white

108

potatoes, glistening with oil and sparkling with salt, cloves of garlic squeezed in between them at regular intervals.

"Great. I'll be back in a sec and I'll put the coffee on."

I head to the toilet and ponder where Jonathan has gone. Sam said he's meeting Janie after work so presumably Jon isn't with her. Or maybe he is at the moment and they're talking things through. Hopefully by the time Sam sees his sister she will be feeling happier.

My gut feeling really is that Jonathan isn't interested in Lydia and genuinely does want things to work with Janie. I think I know him well enough to be a reasonably good judge of these things.

When I return to the kitchen, Julie is just shutting the oven doors and she's already got the coffee on the go.

"You are so efficient," I say.

"That's me. I really do miss it. I love, love, love being a mum, but I think I need something for me, too. And although I'm happy working with you to run this place you know it's not my passion. My heart is in the kitchen," she adds in a terrible Italian accent.

"You'd better not leave it here," I say. "Jonathan might cook it."

"True. One more reason to make this place all-veggie."

I pour us both some coffee and stir in a little cream with a sprinkle of brown sugar. "Shall we take these outside?"

"Sounds good. It looks so nice out there. That is one bonus of not being wedged into a kitchen all the time; I get to appreciate the beautiful weather."

"We should think about it, though – what you want to do, I mean. I know it's more complicated now, with Jon involved, but this is your business – yours and mine, I mean. If you want to be back here then you should be."

"It would mean leaving Zinnia, though."

I push open the door with my bum, and stand back to let Julie out into the vivid daylight. Meg, who has been lying on the warm gravel in the sunshine, stands up slowly, stretches her front legs and gives a wide yawn then trots up to us, her tail wagging lazily. I follow her and Julie across the gravel.

"But if Luke really is able to give up the London time, maybe you and he can work out something between you. I remember when Sam had parental leave when Ben was little. Not that it would be the same as that but I really think it did him a lot of good, and Ben. They had so much time together. I felt a bit left out, sometimes."

"Yeah, that was a great thing for Sam to do," Julie muses. "And it would be good for Luke, and Zinnia. I don't feel like he has bonded the same way she and I have, because he's away so much. But would Zinnia hate it?"

"She'd be OK, I'm sure of it. Maybe not at first but it's like anything – like leaving your baby at nursery. God, that was awful, when Ben went through a phase of crying and clinging on to me, but they sent me a video ten minutes after I'd gone and he was sitting on someone's knee, being read to, happy as Larry. I'm sure they try it on, these kids."

"Ha! Probably. I bet Zinnia's actually legging it round the house after we've all gone to bed and just pretending she doesn't know how to walk so I'll carry her everywhere. But back to this place… I don't really know that I can come back, and push Jon's nose out of joint."

"I know. It's a really tricky one. But I do wonder if he's going to decide he needs to move on sometime soon."

"Really?"

"Yes…" I fill her in on everything that's happened, from Sam telling me that he thought Janie was unhappy, to Jonathan confiding in me and, finally, Lydia.

110

"Bloody Lydia," Julie says.

"I know. Well, kind of. But she's just looking out for herself, isn't she?"

"Yes, she is! And that's the problem. You'd normally be raging about something like this."

"I suppose I would. And I do feel very sympathetic towards Janie. She does seem to have become more insular lately. And less confident. The last thing she needs is Jon's beautiful, self-assured ex-girlfriend arriving back in town and shaking things up."

"Well, yeah. Not to mention Lydia's trying to nick our business."

"There is that." I smile. "But I just don't feel too badly about it. I may be wrong but I don't think it's her – I think it's *Felicity*. It seems to me that she's got a lot of connections – including Paul, as it turns out – and I feel like she's trying to do what we do but on a more... *upmarket*... kind of scale. All her writing tutors, you know, they're high-profile people from that media kind of world. Not lovely local Vanessa and Rosie – and that's not me belittling them at all. I just have a feeling Felicity has stolen our idea but not that she is trying to steal our clientele. I don't think they're her type of people, to be honest."

"OK. I'll take your word for it."

"Well, I'm not sure but that's the feeling I get. Mind you, I'm not happy that they tried to nick Shona. She couldn't have done their PR and ours. Too many conflicts of interest."

"I wonder if she turned down a hefty pay-rise in saying no to them?" Julie muses.

"Do you think so? I suppose she might have. That's a nice thought – that she's loyal to us."

"To be fair, I don't think she and Paul are too strapped for cash."

"No!" I laugh. "But I do feel on edge, Julie, and I don't want to. I should be feeling happy, for god's sake! I'm getting married in two weeks' time and we've put an offer in on that house today!"

"Have you?" Julie looks at once interested and a little bit sad. "You know I'm going to miss you, when you go."

"I know. I'll miss you, too. But it's different these days, isn't it? It's not just you and me. It's Sam and Luke, and Ben and Zinnia, and Sophie when she's here."

"And you, Meg," Julie rubs the dog's head and Meg pushes her nose gratefully into my friend's hand. "Maybe we should get a dog, too," says Julie. "Then if Luke's away it will be extra company for me."

"You definitely should. But you know that we're always around, too – and we'll have a spare room. You can come and stay. That is, if we get the house." I don't want to count my chickens before they're hatched.

"I might just do that," says Julie. "But anyway, back to Jonathan, and Janie. And Sam. You say he's meeting Janie after work?"

"Something like that. I don't really know." I show her Sam's brief, hollow text.

"He does seem a bit pissed off," Julie says. "That doesn't sound like him."

"I know, and just when I thought he was coming through his gloominess," I moan. "Bloody hell, why did I have to get tangled up in all this?"

"I'd hardly say you're tangled up. Jonathan's talked to you because you're his friend. Janie's talking to Sam because she's his sister. I tell you, it's Lydia that's the problem. You need to stop being so nice about her."

"Maybe. It's the Sophie thing though, as well, isn't it? I really think that's at the heart of Sam's unhappiness."

"They had a good time while she was back though, didn't they?"

"Yes. They had a great time. He just misses her. And she's so grown up, isn't she? Just think, she's only a couple of years younger than we were when we came down here for our golden summer!"

"Wow, yeah, you're right. But he needs to sort it out! He's marrying the best woman in the world in a week or two. How can he be anything less than happy?"

"I don't think he sees me as the best woman in the world at the moment."

"Of course he does. He's just being an idiot. Maybe he's nervous, too. I remember Luke behaving weirdly before we got married."

"Did he?"

"Yeah! Even more than normal! That reminds me, we ought to have a hen party. We could have it at home, and the boys could have a night out. What do you reckon?"

"I hadn't even thought about stag and hen dos. Yes, we should definitely do that. But why do they get to go out?"

"Because you know they'd manage to wake the kids up and I don't really want Zinnia having to deal with a load of drunken men. If we stay in, your mum can come, and Karen—" I pull a face and Julie laughs, "—don't be mean. You'll have both grandmothers on hand should Ben need anything."

"Ooh yeah, I like your thinking."

"Great. I'll sort it. Next weekend? If Jon can hold the fort here?"

"Perfect. I can't imagine Sam inviting him to his stag do, the way things are right now."

"It'll all come out in the wash," Julie laughs. "Whatever that means."

113

I sit back, feeling the sun warm my face and the bare skin of my arms. The line of trees is at its most brilliant, springlike green and when I close my eyes briefly I focus in on the birdsong, permeating the air from all directions. I hear a distant high-pitched cry and open my eyes to look up, searching the limitless blue sky until I focus on three buzzards, so high above that they are little more than dots, swirling in lazy circles on the currents.

I feel better for talking to Julie, as I knew I would. Whatever's going on in my life, I can always talk to her, and I never doubt that she's got my back.

16

When Sam gets back, it's late and I'm sitting in bed reading. He missed teatime and Ben's bath- and bed-times but he did at least text to say he was going to.

"Hello," I say in my best cheery, nothing-to-see-here kind of voice.

"Hi." His reply is flat.

"How's Janie?" I ask, laying my book open on top of the duvet and shuffling back so I'm sitting a little straighter.

"As you'd expect," he says.

"Upset?"

"Yep."

"What a nightmare."

"Yep."

I take a deep breath. I have had enough. "Sam, you do know this is nothing to do with me, don't you? I haven't made Lydia come back. I haven't facilitated her and Jonathan keeping in touch – and, I might add, I really don't think it has been much more than the odd email, and nor has it been initiated by Jonathan. Come on," I say, suddenly thinking of Sam's own situation, "what about you and Kate? She's your ex. You're in contact with her all the time."

"We have a daughter," he says superciliously.

"Yes, you do, but that's not the point." I wonder briefly if, actually, that is the point. But no. I won't have this. "Have I ever made you feel bad about keeping in touch with Kate?"

"What about when you found out about Sophie?" Sam tries a little lamely.

"Yes, because you hadn't told me about her."

"Exactly." This isn't making any sense. "You were annoyed because I hadn't told you, and now you haven't told me, about Jonathan and Lydia."

"Argh!" I say, slapping my book down onto my bedside table. "Sam, this is ridiculous. I don't know what this argument is about or why it even *is*, to be honest. I didn't tell you about 'Jonathan and Lydia' because I really don't think there is any 'Jonathan and Lydia'. Yes, I wish I had told you what Lydia said to me… I really wish I'd told you that," I murmur more to myself than him, "but I didn't, because I had a feeling you would overreact. Like you're doing now."

This is the worst type of argument. There is no clear line to follow. I try to put it into some sort of order in my head so that I can sort this out. Annoyingly, I find I am close to tears. I just can't help but think about how we're getting married so soon and that this should be a happy time for us.

"But he's messing my sister about."

"He isn't. He really isn't. At worst, I think, he is guilty of not telling her that Lydia and he had been in touch with each other. I honestly, truly, do not believe anything is going on between Jonathan and Lydia. I honestly, truly, believe that Jon loves Janie and wants her to be happy."

"He's got a funny way of showing it," Sam huffs.

"Oh Sam, I don't get it. I don't, really, know why you are so angry about all this."

He pulls off his jeans, climbs under the duvet, but is careful not to touch me in any way. I hate, hate, hate this feeling.

"Sam," I try a different tack. "Please talk to me. Tell me what Janie said to you."

"I don't know if I should."

"OK. You want to keep her confidence. I get that. But is she OK? Does she think that Jon's been cheating on her?"

"No." Sam seems to deflate, and he sighs. "At least, not now. I told her, what you'd said, about Jonathan."

"Really?" I am pleasantly surprised and think I recognise a tiny glimmer of hope.

"Yeah. I do believe, really, that there's nothing going on with him. And I know Lydia's been in London all this time. But now she's back…"

"Yes, she is. And that is up to her. But whatever her intentions may or may not be, Jonathan loves your sister. I am sure of it. He's not like he was in the old days. He's grown up."

I think of Jon now and wonder where he was this afternoon and evening. What was the family emergency? A horrible shadow of doubt crosses my mind, in the shape of Lydia. I banish it.

"I hope you're right."

"Come on, Sam. I think you know I am." I hope I am.

"I said to Janie," he's starting to open up now, "that she needs to talk to him. Not just about Lydia, but about life. Their life together. The future."

"Sounds sensible." I don't want to say too much. I feel like I need to listen now.

"Yeah, well, I think they're in a bit of a sticky situation. I don't think she's happy here, to be honest. But she wants to be with him."

"That's the impression that I got from Jon," I say, pleased to be aligning myself with Sam now. My eagerness to agree with him irritates me but still, I am so desperate for us to be happy. For him to be happy. I want him to know I am on his side. Always.

"It's difficult, though, isn't it? His career. His passion for what he does, and where."

I'd never really thought Sam had noticed this about Jonathan before.

"It reminds me of Christian," he says. "And I know how much blood, sweat and tears went into the Cross-Section. He couldn't have had a relationship, not then. He barely can now, it's just lucky Sadie's so chilled out about the whole thing."

"Yeah. God, I wouldn't want to be with a chef. No offence to Julie!" I think how my friend has put her career to the side, though, in favour of family life. Could Jonathan do that, for the good of his relationship? Would he want to? He's just building up his reputation. The pop-up kitchen at Amethi is getting rave reviews and is booking up months ahead. I know he hopes it's a stepping stone, to his own place. But how would that work with Janie? I don't know. And actually, I remind myself, I don't have to. I care very much about them both but this is not my problem to solve. Nor is it Sam's.

"Did Janie go home, after you'd seen her?"

"Yeah. She was going to go to Mum's but I told her not to. I said she should sort things out with Jon."

"Good." The last person Janie needs advice from, I think, is Karen. I have become very fond of my almost-mother-in-law and she's softened quite a lot since she's been back – particularly when it comes to Ben – but even so, I wouldn't look to her for relationship advice. "Now tell me, Sam, why you're so angry with me, please."

He sighs. "I'm not. Not really. I'm sorry, Alice. I'm…" His eyes fill with tears.

"What is it?" I ask, suddenly awash with concern. This is not like Sam. Not at all.

"It's Sophie," he says.

"Is she OK?"

"She's fine!" he laughs humourlessly. "Totally fine. But she's not coming back this summer."

"What?" The plan has always been that Sophie would be here over the summer holidays. She was last year and it was lovely. It's so busy for Isaac and Kate anyway, and where they live is so remote that it could be incredibly boring for Sophie. She isn't old enough to drive, so she's essentially stuck on that hillside – beautiful though it is – with her mum, her stepdad, and her toddler brother. At least here she can be straight out into town, meeting up with her old friends, and of course spending some proper time with Sam. Last summer was beautiful because it was unhurried, and so relaxed.

"Yeah," he says glumly. "She says she'll be here for the solstice and our wedding. As if she's doing us a favour."

"Sam," I say warningly at his bitter tone.

"But that she'd prefer to be in Devon for the summer holidays. Some of her older mates have got cars – that gives you an idea of the kids she's hanging out with; got their own cars at seventeen, eighteen – and will pick her up. They've got it all planned out. Surfing, beach parties… basically all the stuff she can do here. Told me on the phone earlier, just after I called the estate agent."

"Oh, Sam." I squash down my urge to ask if he has heard back from Roger; I don't suppose that would be very sensitive. "No wonder you're pissed off."

"Yeah. I don't know why I didn't see this coming. And it's not that I don't love you and Ben, so completely. You know I do."

"Of course I know that. But it doesn't make you love Sophie any less."

"No." His eyes meet mine properly for the first time since he's been back. "I'm just starting to feel more and more redundant. Surplus to her life. When she was little, and she never knew I wasn't her real dad, I felt like I was the world to her. Me and Kate, of course. She wanted to be with me, all the time. She loved all the things I did, and she wanted to do the work I do. Now she's not interested really. She wants to study psychology," I detect the merest hint of disdain in his voice, which I think is unfair – and I actually think it's good that Sophie's got her own interests, but I don't voice this – "and she just doesn't seem to need me anymore."

"Sam," I say, and I put my arm around his shoulder, pull his head gently to my chest. "Of course she needs you. This is so normal, you know. When I was Sophie's age, the last thing I wanted to do was be like my mum and dad. Now, I see what amazing people they are and I like it when people say I share some of their characteristics. But when you're sixteen, do you really want to be compared to your old-codger parents?'

"I don't suppose you do," Sam says.

"The thing is, Karen left for Spain when you were that age. You were independent because you had to be. To loads of kids that age, your situation might seem really attractive. You could do what you liked, when you liked – even if you were living with your aunty at first, it doesn't sound like she was particularly strict – while a lot of teenagers have family homes which to them seem full of unnecessary rules and restrictions. Just when you want your freedom, you feel like you're being held back. I think," I am getting into my stride now and hoping this doesn't sound too much like a lecture, "that you have to let Sophie do this and, more than let her, support her. Be interested in what she's doing. Let her have her freedom, but also make sure she knows you are here – *we* are here – for her, whenever and whatever."

"She does know that. I always tell her that," Sam sniffs.

"Good. And I know it's hard but you have to try not to let this feel like a reflection on your relationship with her. She's a good girl and she loves you. She'll come back and hopefully as she gets older she'll come back more and more. But she's been through some tough times and it can't be easy having two homes, and two sets of friends. She won't want to be missing out, Sam. That's the thing. If she misses the summer; all those parties and beach days, when she goes back to Devon in September she'll feel it badly."

"OK," Sam pulls himself up and kisses me on the cheek. "You've convinced me. You're quite a wise woman, aren't you?"

"I like to think so."

"I'm sorry for being so arsey earlier."

"Well," I don't know what to say but I think I should apologise too. "I'm sorry, Sam, as well. I wasn't keeping secrets from you, I promise. Well, I was, but not because I wanted to. But it felt like it wasn't my secret to tell."

"I get that," he says.

"Let's hope they work it out, eh?"

"Yeah. And can you remind me, of all that stuff about Sophie, when I get grumpy again?"

"You won't be grumpy, though," I smile and I kiss him. "Because you'll be married to the most wonderful, wise woman, won't you?"

"You've got a point," he kisses me back. "And my sister had better sort out her shit before the wedding because nobody and nothing is going to ruin that."

17

The next day, all is quiet at Amethi when I arrive for work. I walk as gently as possible across the gravel, noticing that the curtains are closed in Jonathan and Janie's house. I experience a moment of nostalgic longing, for the time when I lived there. On my own at first, then with Sam, and eventually with Sophie, too. When Ben was on his way, we realised we couldn't stay there any longer. It would have been too much of a squeeze. But I loved that place. The peace, the quiet. The age and history.

I used to imagine what Amethi was like in its heyday – or 'hayday' as my dad has joked more than once… it used to be a farm… get it? – when the little house was a barn. Keeping animals safe and dry in the winter, the air filled with that familiar warm sweet scent of lived-in hay, and clouds of breath from velvety nostrils as the creatures huddled together in the cold of the night.

I've always loved a place with a sense of history and so it's come as a surprise to me that I feel so drawn towards the new house, which can be no more than ten or twelve years old. I'm just waiting on Sam to call me, though, and tell me what the response is to our offer. As had become apparent once the atmosphere had thawed between Sam and me yesterday, Roger had not yet phoned back.

"I will ring him, if he hasn't called by lunchtime," Sam said this morning, before kissing me goodbye.

"Bye, Mummy," Ben had said, down by Sam's legs, his chubby little hand holding his nursery bag like a briefcase.

"Are you off to work as well, Benny?" I crouched down

so I could kiss and hug him. "You go and make lots of money, OK?"

"No, I'm going to nursery, silly!" he had laughed.

"Oh, I see. Well, be a good boy, won't you? I'll miss you but I'll see you this afternoon."

He put his arms around my neck and I pulled him to me, inhaling his little-boy aroma: last night's bubble bath, combined with the fresh, minty smell of toothpaste and a vague scent of the Weetabix he had for breakfast.

I head on over to the office, noting the heavy grey clouds suspended to the west. They look like they're coming this way. Still, it's warm enough and when I get to the little office at the top of the stairs and open the door, it's like the heat has been trapped up there, just awaiting its release. It rushes me as I walk in and I open the window in front of my desk, inhaling the fresh air, which carries a subtle floral sweetness.

I sit down and I am soon ensconced in the world of answering bookings and enquiries. It keeps me busy for a good hour and takes my mind off all that happened yesterday. I hope Jonathan and Janie managed to sort out their troubles. There has been no sign of Jon yet so maybe they're having a lazy morning. He's often in the kitchen in the morning but he doesn't really need to be there till the afternoon. He and Julie have it all covered in terms of ordering food, setting menus and so on, Julie often working from home rather than coming up to Amethi; fitting in emails and phone calls while Zinnia has a nap, or is held to Julie's right hip. I do miss my friend's company while I'm here. Just like those days of living in the cottage here, I often look back to pre-children times, when we were working so many hours to make a success of this place. We would both be in the office most days, Julie's familiar presence a constant and a comfort. But we have to change just as our lives have; adapt as necessary. It is hard but it works, somehow.

Just as I'm checking over the last of the responses to possible booking enquiries, my phone goes. It's Sam.

"Hello?" I answer as I press 'send' and watch the email vanish from my screen.

"Hi Alice," his tone does not sound buoyant. I guess our offer's been rejected. I don't know if we'll be able to go any higher. My heart sinks before Sam's had a chance to say anything. "Is Jon there?"

"Jon? No. Do you want to speak to him?"

"I… no, not really. I just wondered if he's OK. I had a call from Janie just now and she went back to Mum's last night, instead of going home."

"Oh. Oh no." I think of the closed curtains in the cottage. Not such a good sign, after all.

"Yeah. I don't know why she didn't just go back home. But anyway, she's at Mum's at the moment."

"What about her computer?"

"That's at the cottage. She asked me to get it for her."

"What? Really?"

"M-hmm. I'm not really sure what's going on."

"Do you want me to go and see if Jon's about?"

"It might be a good idea."

"You don't think he's done anything…?" My mind flits to Jonathan's absence yesterday afternoon. A family emergency or something else? And by 'something else' I mean Lydia.

"Honestly, I don't know. All Janie would say was that she needs some space."

"Right." That old chestnut. "I'll go and knock on the cottage door. I don't suppose…"

"Roger's called? No, not yet. I will tell you as soon as he does," I hear a slight smile in Sam's voice now. "I promise."

"And you'll call him if he hasn't called you?"

"By lunchtime… yes."

"OK. I'll go and see if I can find out what's going on."

Meg is in her usual place, lying out at the side of the building, her eyes half-closed and chest moving with her heavy breath.

"Are you hot, girl?" Silly question. The sky is still moody and brooding but if anything it is hotter today than it was yesterday. Nevertheless, when she sees me, Meg gets to her feet and trots along at my side as I head for the cottage.

Knock, knock.

Nothing.

The curtains are still closed upstairs.

"Jon?" I try, tentatively, but hopefully loud enough that he can hear me if he's in there. That's a point. What if he's not? What if neither he nor Janie came back last night?

Images of Lydia and Jonathan together flood my mind… I remember the way they used to look at each other when they worked together at the Sail Loft. A memory of the two of them, dancing at Stef and April's wedding… they were so happy.

But it was a long time ago. And I think of Jonathan and Janie, and how they seem when they're together – or at least how they have seemed, until recently. That Christmas when Jon was so unhappy and then Karen and Janie had turned up, out of the blue. She'd gone back to Spain but had come back to Cornwall, to be with him. Which is part of the problem, I think – she came back because she wanted to be with him, not because she wanted to be here.

There is no answer now. No twitch of the curtains. No sign of life, in fact. I have an idea and I scurry round to the car park, Meg hot on my heels.

Phew. It's there, the car. Jon's car. Which means he must be at home, and I guess is still in bed. In which case, I should leave him be. He won't need to be in the kitchen till after lunch and he has every right to stay in bed, resting, or wallowing, or whatever he likes. I'm well aware of the extra pressure that comes from living where you work, and I'm very keen that Jonathan should not feel like I expect him to be at my beck and call.

Before I go back into the office, I sit on the gravel, leaning against the wall, Meg leaning against me. Her body is moving in time with her panting and I smooth the fur from the bony lump at the top of her head, all the way down her back, till she sinks down onto her belly.

"Good girl. You stay here and I'll be back down at lunchtime. We'll go for a…"

I let the sentence tail off before I let the word 'walk' slip past my lips into the open air. Once that's out, there is no taking it back. Still, Meg seems happy to be here at Amethi, with the run of the place. She is popular with the guests and often gets them throwing her ball for her. Occasionally, we will have somebody who is less than keen on dogs, or even scared of them. When this is the case, I keep her with me, in the office when I'm in there, or else on a lead if we're out walking near the holiday lets. She really is as good as gold and while she's not company in the same way that Julie is, she is a pleasure to have around.

By lunchtime, there is still no sign of Jonathan, and no word yet from Sam – so presumably he hasn't heard from Roger. I go downstairs, stepping gratefully into the humid air. It may be warm out here but it's close to suffocating in the office. The fan we put in is both a blessing and a curse – cooling the air but also blowing papers around. It's not conducive to a successful morning's work.

Meg stands to greet me and shakes herself, her whole body wagging along with her tail.

"Hello, girl," I put my hand out to her. "Shall we go for a walk?"

We set off towards the meadows and I sneak a look back towards the holiday lets and the cottage. The curtains are still closed in Jon and Janie's place. If there's no sign of him when I get back, I'm going to have to knock again, because Jonathan will need to get to work, to make sure all our guests are catered for on time. This is part of the selling point with Amethi. A private chef, cooking meals to order for guests to enjoy in the privacy of their holiday homes. I think briefly of the Bay Hotel, pleased that they can't really compete on this level. And we pride ourselves on being as flexible as possible here, trying to fulfil as many wishes of the guests as we can, as long as they're not too outlandish.

As I walk along the dry, cracked path at the edge of the field, towards the woods, Meg scampers ahead, sniffing at the hedgerows and alert to all sounds from the undergrowth and the woods ahead. There's a badger sett there, which I hope Meg never disturbs. I don't fancy her chances against an angry badger.

We wander along and I think of Sam, and how sad he was last night. How sad he's been, really. I can't imagine how it would feel if Ben lived away and lost interest in seeing me. At the moment, I am spoiled by his evident joy at the sight of me. I know it can't last forever. I am destined to become embarrassing, and stupid, as he grows up. He'll think I know nothing, as though I only came into existence when he did. No past of my own; no younger days when I might have been cool (I don't think I ever achieved that, really). I remember feeling like that about my mum and dad, like they didn't understand what it was like to be a teenager. It's the natural order of things. A rite of passage for kids. But I suspect very painful – not to mention annoying – for parents.

As we enter the woods, the air becomes cooler. Above us, jackdaws squawk and squabble from their lofty perches high up in the branches. A squirrel darts hurriedly away, scooting up the nearest tree and as far away from Meg and me as possible. On a sunny day, I love the way the sunlight filters through the leaves and dapples the floor but today all is dark and moody; it feels almost like dusk in the shade of the woods.

Meg knows the way; our regular lunchtime ramble, which only takes about fifteen minutes but gives me the chance to clear my head. Then I have fifteen minutes more to have something to eat, before it's back to work. I'm strict about making sure I have a break – and strict about not letting it run on too long. As we circle along the woodland path, I am startled by a figure. Hunched up, at the base of a tree. Jonathan.

"Jon!" I exclaim. "Are you OK?"

He looks up, his eyes red and his face pale.

"Alice," he says, though it's like he's not really seeing me.

"Are you OK?" I ask again. "Are you hurt?"

"No. No, I'm fine. Sorry. I just came out for a walk."

"OK." This does not look like a walk to me. Meg approaches him, sniffing his face and licking his ear. This does at least produce a small smile. He reaches out to her, strokes her chest.

"Jon," I say gently. "Sam told me Janie stayed at Karen's last night."

"Yeah," he says. "I think she's had enough of me."

"Really?" I want to ask what he means. And I want to know where he was yesterday afternoon. But I need to tread carefully. "Are you coming back soon? I'm going to go back for lunch. Do you want something?"

"I'm fine, thanks," he says, "don't worry about me. I'll be over there soon, though. I know there's lots to do."

"There is," I acknowledge. "But only if you're feeling up to it."

"Yeah. I am." He heaves himself to his feet. "Sorry. Just feeling sorry for myself."

"That's OK. It's fine. Is there anything I can help with?"

"No, it's messy enough as it is. Thank you, though, Alice."

I wait while he makes his way gingerly through the undergrowth to my side, then we walk together, Meg trotting ahead again.

"Want to talk about it?"

"I… I don't know. I just feel like shit. I don't blame Janie for staying away."

"But why?" I can't help asking.

"I don't know. I get like this sometimes." He shrugs. "Sometimes something triggers it, and sometimes it just creeps up on me."

"So it's not just about you and Janie?"

"No. It's not. But things aren't great, Alice. You must know that. Sometimes I think I should just make it easy for her. Be a bastard so she can leave me, get on with her life."

"But she loves you, Jon. And you love her."

"Is it that simple, though? Is it enough?"

I don't answer. I know what he means, I think. When Sam had gone to study in Wales, I'd thought love was definitely enough. But then life, and circumstances, dictated something different. Sophie needed him, more than I did. I came to realise that. But on the surface, Jon's and Janie's situation is far more simple.

"You can make it work, Jon, if you want to. I'm sure of it."

"You've got faith in me," he smiles sadly. "Thank you. I'm just so tired, though. I don't know if I can give her what she needs."

And has Lydia got anything to do with this? I want to ask, but I also feel like that would belittle this situation, somehow. It seems to me this is not some silly story about an ex turning up and rocking the boat. Maybe it goes much further back than that. Again, I remember how down Jonathan had been, and despondent, that winter a couple of years ago. Sure that he'd never progress in his career, or find love, or have a family, if he stayed. Lydia had broken his heart and he doubted himself much more than I had realised he could. On first appearances, he is confident and full of himself; in fact, I didn't like him much at all to begin with. But there is more to him than that.

Then came Janie, and the move from the Sail Loft to Amethi. To the cottage. It occurs to me now that maybe these aren't exactly the answers he needed.

As we emerge from the canopy of trees back into the murky daylight, as if reading my mind he says, "I've come full circle, Alice, only I feel like it's messier than ever. I've got Lydia calling me, wanting to meet up, which is driving me mad. And Janie disappointed in me because I can't give her what she wants. I love working here, with you and Julie – you know that – but the years are passing by, Alice, and I want something of my own. Don't think I'm ungrateful please but here I am, living in a borrowed house, working in a borrowed job. I couldn't even meet a girlfriend independently – she's your boyfriend's sister, for god's sake!"

"But that doesn't matter. I mean, how do people meet each other? If not through friends, or work? It's better than a drunken hook-up. And she loves you." He smiles thinly but I carry on. "She does! And yes, I do get what you're saying, about needing your own things. Your own place. I mean, look at me and Sam. I rented from David then we lived here, then at Mum and Dad's house, now we're living at Luke and Julie's." I don't mention that we are trying to buy our own home now. "And until Julie and I found Amethi, I was managing Bea's business. We had some luck here, too. With Paul Winters, I mean. If he hadn't done what he did in making sure we could get this place, we might still be looking. I might still be at the Sail Loft! Working for my parents."

Jon looks like he's considering all of this. I bump gently against his side. "Thank you for telling me how you're feeling."

"I feel a bit better for talking to you," he says, and manages a real smile.

"I'm glad. But you know, if you do find it difficult managing your feelings sometimes, it wouldn't hurt to talk to a doctor. They're not going to just put you on pills or anything like that."

"Yeah, maybe," he says, but I'm not convinced.

"Why don't you go home, have a shower or freshen up—" I sound like my mum, "—and I'll get some lunch ready for us. It won't be anything flash, mind, so don't go judging me. You know I'm a crap cook. You could give Janie a ring, too," I suggest, but I leave it at that. It's up to Jon now.

"Thank you, Alice. I'll do that. I'll be back soon."

We walk quietly along the side of the meadow, disturbing an Emperor butterfly that had been warming its wings in the sun. Then Jonathan heads for home while I walk back across to the kitchen, Meg by my side. I get her a fresh bowl of water, which she laps at gratefully before sinking onto her side again.

Inside, I put the kettle on and find half a quiche in the fridge. I slice it then chop up some tomatoes, onion, cucumber and radish, drop some salad leaves onto two plates, and assemble the chopped veg on top, drizzling the lot with dressing. Two small slices of quiche each, and a jug of water, ice and lemon bobbing merrily on the surface. I take the whole lot out to one of the tables.

Presently, Jonathan returns. He looks a bit better, his hair wet from – presumably – a shower, and clothes clean and fresh. "This looks good," he says, gesturing to the plates.

"Don't patronise me!" I chance a joke and I'm glad to see him smile properly. It's like the sun breaking through on a misty day. I want to ask if he's spoken to Janie but he will tell me if he wants to. For now, I'm just glad he's back with me.

We tuck into our lunch and Jon pours us both a glass of water. We clink glasses in a silent *cheers*. I sip my drink and look out across the meadows, towards the trees. Between Sam and Jon, I think, I don't know who's been more of a misery lately. I allow myself a small slice of satisfaction that I seem to have managed to cheer them both up.

18

My smug smile only grows when Sam calls, to tell me that our offer has been accepted.

"We're going to be home-owners!" I say.

"Well, us and the bank... and really, the bank more than us. For the next twenty-five years."

"Alright, alright, don't ruin the moment!"

"It's good isn't it, Alice?" His voice is soft and happy.

"Yes. It is."

"I never thought I'd be bothered about stuff like this but I don't know, I just feel like it makes us authentic. A real family. I know, I know, we are already a real family, and would be, whatever the situation we found ourselves living in. And it's really just society's expectations that I'm trying to live up to. I know all that, and yet it feels good."

"I know exactly what you mean. And we're getting married... something else I didn't think would ever happen. And again, it doesn't change anything, in a way. But I just feel so happy, and so lucky."

I think of Jon when I found him, hunched on the ground by the tree. I may have made him feel a little better today but I'm not stupid. I know his problems can't be solved just like that.

"Me too, Alice. Me too."

"I spoke to Jon today, you know."

"Oh yeah?"

"Yes. I don't know what's going on, exactly. I think the problems there are deeper than this situation with Lydia."

"Oh yeah?"

"I… can't really say too much, but I think it would be good if Janie came back and she and Jon talked more about it all."

I can almost hear the change in Sam – suddenly bristling, thinking I'm criticising Janie. He's so defensive when it comes to her, and to Sophie – but hopefully that means he's the same when it comes to me.

"It's nothing she's done," I say quickly. "I don't really think it's anything Jon's done, either, you know. I think he's really sad and he wants things to be good between the two of them."

"And Lydia?"

"Honestly, Sam, I really don't think she comes into it. She's a minor player. An irritation. Jon's…" What can I say, without breaking Jonathan's confidence? I'm touched that he trusted me today. "Jon's having a hard time," I finish.

"OK." Sam sounds suspicious but I think he knows I don't want to say anything more. "Look, I've got to get back to work. Hopefully Janie'll head home today anyway but if she doesn't, I'll go round to Mum's – maybe take Ben over – and just see if I can find out what's going on."

"That's a great idea," I say, relieved he doesn't sound so aggrieved at Jonathan.

"Maybe I'll see if they want to come down to the beach, for a little picnic?" he muses, warming to the idea.

"That sounds lovely," I say, thinking it also means I might get some time to myself after work. Bonus!

When I pop down to see Jon during the afternoon, he's zipping about the kitchen, from hob to oven to chopping board; somehow keeping four different meals on the go, whereas I struggle to make just one salad without some kind of disaster.

"Have you phoned Janie?" I ask him, mock-nonchalantly, while I pour myself some iced water.

"No, I… thought I'd wait till I've got all this lot done. Make sure everything's OK here then hopefully I'll be able to focus on her, and on us."

"That sounds sensible," I say.

"I don't want to drag her down. Or stop her doing what she wants to do."

"I get that. I don't think you are, though – dragging her down, I mean. I do think maybe you should have told her about Lydia."

"Yeah, I know. I'm an idiot."

"No, no," I rush to try and reassure him. I realise just how much he needs his confidence right now. "I get why you didn't. It's one of those things, isn't it? I'm just as bad. I always know I should say things to Sam, and just be open – and that not doing it will make more problems. But sometimes it's hard to find the right moment, isn't it?"

"Yeah," he looks at me almost gratefully.

"Life's complicated sometimes."

"You can say that again."

"You'll work it out, Jon. I know it."

"I hope so."

I go outside to drink my water, sitting on the gravel in the shade next to Meg, just soaking in the sunshine and peace. It seems most of the guests are out at the moment – no doubt making the most of the beaches in this premium time, when the weather is at its best, the days at their longest, and the kids are still in school.

This might be my favourite time; my favourite month of my favourite season. The apex of spring. It's hard to believe that this season started out so gloomy and moody. It makes me hopeful that life will change again, for

135

Jonathan and Janie, and for Sam and Sophie. They need to find their way through these tricky situations. I turn my face to the sun and hope for happier times.

19

By Saturday, things do seem more settled and I'm starting to feel excited about my hen do. Which takes my mind off feeling nervous about my fast-approaching wedding.

"Luke's taking you and Meg up to Jim's," Julie tells Sam.

He raises his eyebrow, used to being told what to do by my friend (which doesn't necessarily mean he always obeys).

"At about two," she says. "But I have to go and get some… thing first."

Sam looks at me and I shrug. I am in the dark about all this and have happily let Julie get on with organising the day's events. She insisted on looking after Ben this morning and bringing breakfast to me and Sam while we were still in bed.

"Consider it an early wedding present," she said, shepherding Ben out of the room; recognising his intention of climbing up and bouncing on his mum and dad. "And I won't get many more chances to do this, when you're in your own place," she added with a mock-sad face.

"Julie, I don't think you have ever done this before," I said, "and we've lived here over a year."

"But thank you, Julie," Sam said, nudging me.

"Well yes, of course, thank you!"

"My pleasure." She cast her sweetest smile our way then turned to Ben. "Come on, Benny boy, I'll race you back to the lounge. We've left Zinnia. Maybe she'll be up on her feet and dancing when we get back."

There followed the sound of giggling and two pairs of feet – one large, one small – running down the stairs.

Sam turned to me. "This is so nice," he said. "She's outdone herself."

The breakfast tray was covered with a patterned cloth, which Sam pulled back to reveal warm croissants, a mini butter dish and little pots of jam and marmalade, as well as freshly cut pineapple, and a pot of coffee alongside a jug of warm milk and two blue-and-white striped mugs. One says 'Mr' and one says 'Mrs'.

I hope that's not tempting fate," I said, turning them for Sam to see.

"I don't think so. Nothing's going to stop me marrying you."

"What if I change my mind?"

"You won't," he smiled.

"Feeling confident, are we?"

"Yes. I am. Although I'm a bit worried about you tonight. Didn't Julie get that policeman strip-o-gram for Bea on her hen do?"

"Urgh, she did. But she wouldn't do that to me. Not here. Not with our kids in the house. And she knows I'd kill her if she pulled a stunt like that."

"Well, just be careful," Sam grinned.

"I will. I'm hoping for a nice genteel evening of cocktails and polite conversation."

"Me too."

"I thought so. Do you know what Luke's got planned?"

"Honestly… I think just a night down the pub. Nothing major. He's knackered. I'm knackered. Most of our mates have got kids and wives these days. We're all knackered, quite frankly."

"All the more reason *you* need to be careful, then. There's bound to be at least one loose cannon. Somebody having relationship troubles…"

I trail off as I think of Jonathan. He's working tonight at Amethi so won't be at Sam's stag do, much to Sam's relief, I think. I was pleased that Jon had at least been invited.

"I might pop down to buy Sam a beer," he'd told me, "after work. But I don't think I'll be stopping. They'll all be wasted by that time anyway. I'll never catch up."

"Not my darling angel Sam," I'd grinned.

"No, of course not."

Janie had come back home that day that I'd talked to Jonathan and, while I haven't wanted to pry or ask too many questions, he's told me that they have been talking a lot more. He has also told Lydia to back off, apparently.

In other circumstances, I'd have gladly invited Lydia to my hen do but of course this is not an option now. Janie will be there, for one thing – for another, I'm still not comfortable with Lydia's motives, in terms of Jonathan and in terms of work.

"They're getting a wedding licence, at the Bay," Julie had reported to me. "Don't you think we should look into that again?"

It had crossed my mind, with thoughts of my own impending nuptials. George's enthusiasm about the Longhouse is catching.

"Go on, then," I'd said. "Let's match them step-for-step. They're nicking our ideas, let's nick theirs."

"Great, I'm on it."

So, in short, I'm avoiding Lydia and hoping she is avoiding Jonathan. It's a shame things have to be this way.

A little before lunchtime, Julie leaves Sam and me with Ben and Zinnia. "Just got to go and get that… thing… I mentioned earlier."

"OK." I raise my eyebrows at Sam, who is holding

Zinnia's hands while she stands.

"She's doing it!" he says.

"Yeah, till you let go of her hands," Julie says. "That girl's destined to be carried everywhere."

Sam gently eases his hands away and Zinnia continues standing. For a moment, and a wobbly moment at that, but it's progress.

"Oh ye of little faith," says Sam.

"Well, I'll be blowed," Julie says, ducking down to give Zinnia a kiss. "Clever girl! I have to dash, though, or I'll be late."

She is gone in a Julie-shaped cloud of dust, leaving me, Sam, Ben, Zinnia and Meg in her wake. Luke apparently also had things to do today so we are slightly nervously holding the fort, hoping that tonight will be OK.

After about twenty minutes, we hear Julie's car outside. Meg moves to the front door, excitedly. She's going to miss Julie when we move to our new place. I think to her we are all her family.

"Who is it, Meg?" I ask and I open the door, to see Julie and none other than Sophie. They both put their fingers to their lips. "Shhhh..!"

I do as I'm told, and I step back. Sam had not been expecting to see his daughter till next weekend. He's going to be so happy. And I am delighted she's come for my hen party.

"Surprise!" Sophie says, bursting into the lounge. Both Sam and Ben look up, and Zinnia starts to cry.

"Oh, I'm sorry!" Sophie exclaims but she is already being engulfed by Sam and Ben's arms, while Julie goes to Zinnia and picks her up.

"I had no idea!" Sam says gruffly, smiling half-shyly, his pleasure evident.

"No, well that was the plan."

"But it's my stag do…" he starts to say.

"And Alice's hen do," Sophie smiles. "I know. That's why I'm here."

"Well, you are very welcome," I say. "In fact, that's made my night."

"It hasn't even begun yet, lady," Julie smiles.

"And I'm taking you for lunch tomorrow, Dad," Sophie says. "Mum and Isaac gave me some money. I hope you don't mind, Alice, but we thought it might be nice if just me and Dad had some time…"

"I don't mind at all. I think it's a great idea."

When Luke gets back, we all sit down to lunch together and I feel so incredibly warm and happy, sitting with all of these people I love so much. Maybe it's the advent of the wedding making me so emotional; I feel tears creeping across my eyes. Sam notices and smiles at me across the table.

"I love you," I mouth to him.

Even Zinnia and Ben manage to behave, eating the food in front of them with practically no objections. Ben insisted on sitting next to Sophie, and he's watching what she's doing, the food she's eating, and trying to emulate her.

Zinnia, too, is fascinated by Sophie. I can see why. She's young, and full of energy, enthusiasm and laughter. She seems so happy and I'm glad.

Despite Sam's and Kate's best efforts, Sophie's life has not always been very settled. To see her now, compared to that younger version, who took herself off to Luke's dad's that Christmastime, making us all think she'd run away – and who went on to confess to having done all sorts of things to keep Sam to herself, messing up our relationship in the process – is almost magical.

As we clear away the dishes, I remark on this, in a less direct way.

"Thank you, Alice. I do feel happy. And I'm really excited about you and Dad getting married!"

"I'm very glad. And so very happy you're here for my hen do!"

"My first one."

"Well, hopefully it won't be too wild."

"I can handle wild."

"I'm sure you can."

Sam and Luke leave at about two, taking Meg with them, as per Julie's instructions. Luke's dad, Jim, has offered to look after Meg, choosing to opt out of the night out. They leave us with kisses and the echo of their laughter as they walk down the drive to Luke's car. As the house readjusts to their absence, Julie lays down the law:

"First, we are going to the beach. We are going to take buckets and spades and swimming stuff and under no circumstances are we allowing Ben or Zinnia to have a nap: we are tiring them out so they go to sleep nice and early and stay that way till morning.

"Next, we come home for an early tea and then get changed, then get the kids to bed. Then out come the drinks, and round come the guests."

All sounds good, and I feel fairly safe that it genuinely will be a quiet, sociable night.

We have a lovely time at the beach and Sophie and Julie insist that I go for a swim.

"Mummy!" I hear Ben's voice calling me. I know he's not that keen on me disappearing into this huge mass of water.

"I'll be fine, Ben," I say. "I'll be back soon."

Sophie distracts him and I jog the rest of the way down to the shore, moving quickly through the gasp of cold. I walk through the waves until it's deep enough to dive in and under the surface, feeling the bubbles moving around me and the salty sting on my eyes and skin. Then I'm up, my head tingling as it breaks the surface and the sun glimmers and glistens on the water all around me. I take strong, luxurious strokes, pushing myself through the oncoming waves and feeling my body move across them. Once I'm far enough out, I turn onto my back, squinting against the sunshine and feeling my hair spread out in the water, like seaweed. I imagine myself half-human, half-sea creature. The swish of the sea fills my ears and the sound of life on land becomes distant; something I am only dimly aware of.

Ben springs to mind but I know he's OK. He's being looked after. Be in the moment, I tell myself. These moments are few and far between these days. I've been so wrapped up in Sam's sadness, and Jonathan and Janie's problems, not to mention planning the solstice week and the wedding, I've forgotten to give myself enough time to just let everything wash over me. Thoughts and feelings settle. I float, lazily sculling my hands every now and then. Watching the occasional gull sail across my field of vision. Behind me is the sun.

I'm getting married, I think. *To Sam*. The man I've loved for what seems like forever. I laugh out loud, the sound mutated in my submerged ears. I quickly look around; check that there is nobody close enough to think I'm mad. Then I turn onto my front and I start to move, strong and steady, side-on to the waves, parallel to the beach. I check where Julie and Sophie are, and see Ben happily playing with his sister. I take the chance to swim, head down and almost oblivious to the other seafarers, glad we chose not to go to the surfers' beach today so I can swim undisturbed by the threat of being mown down by an incoming board.

All the way along I go, till I am close to the rocks at the other end of the beach – then back – and I love every single moment of it. At the shoreline, as I return, I can see Ben and Sophie waving and I know it's time to head in, pick my responsibilities back up, but I feel refreshed and energised, and more than ready to do so.

In the evening, as per Julie's plan, Ben and Zinnia are zonked and they both fall asleep before seven. I kiss Ben's warm forehead and dim his light, shutting the door gently behind me before going to get changed.

I meet up with Julie and Sophie in the lounge, and Julie opens some prosecco. "Sophie, I checked with Kate and Sam and they said you could have one or two glasses, so shall we say two and you can have one of them now?"

"Yes please," Sophie says, and Julie pours the cold, frothing drink into three tall flutes which she's chilled in the fridge.

"Cheers!" she says. "To Alice and Sam."

"To Alice and Sam," Sophie echoes, and we all push our glasses gently together.

Not too long after, my mum arrives, with Sarah. I kiss and hug them both. It would appear they have already had a glass or two before setting off.

Then come Karen, and Janie. "I'll have two daughters soon!" Karen exclaims, pulling me in for a hug.

"And I'll have a sister," Janie smiles.

"I can't wait," I say, and I kiss them both on the cheek. "Come on through, for a drink. Julie's stocked up good and proper. You're not driving, are you?"

"No, I'm staying at Mum's tonight."

"Poor Jon," I say, regretting my choice of words immediately but hurrying blithely on, "working away while the rest of us party. I hope he can meet up with Sam later."

"I hope so," Janie says slightly sadly. "He could do with a bit of a break. I don't mean you work him too hard or anything," she adds hastily.

"I didn't think you did mean that," I reassure her. "Now, come on in. You can always give Jon a ring a bit later to check he's made it out."

"I might do that," she says gratefully.

David turns up soon after. "You came to my hen do," he says, "so it's only right I come to yours."

"I was hoping you would." I kiss him.

"So you're definitely turning down a year in our beautiful house?" he says.

"Yes, I'm afraid so. Lovely as it is. It's time we got our own place."

"I'm really pleased for you."

"I wish you weren't going away, though."

"We'll be back before you know it. And I can't wait to spend some time with Bea. But I will miss you too, Alice."

"Don't add that as an afterthought!" I laugh.

I'm pleased that Julie has kept the guest list minimal. It's just me and most of my favourite women – and David. Julie's made a load of delicious canapes, which she had squirreled away in the freezer in the garage, and I've noticed a load of cocktail-making equipment and piles of booze in the kitchen.

"You've gone to so much trouble," I say, sliding my arm around her shoulder. "Do you think we should start making cocktails?" I'm actually already feeling a little light-headed and have to remind myself that I do have to stay relatively sober for the sake of Ben. And Sophie, for that matter. I can't have her seeing me make a fool of myself.

Julie checks her watch. "Soon…"

She goes to David and whispers something to him, and then the doorbell goes.

Oh no, I think. *She hasn't…*

"I'll get that," Julie says, and sweeps past me. I hear her open the door, and a man's voice. My heart begins beating fast and my face goes red. I can't have a stripper. I would never want one, but particularly not with my mum, and my stepdaughter, and my mother-in-law, and…

"Everyone, this is Ian."

Ian is very good looking, I see. I try to hide behind David, who just laughs and moves out of the way.

"Ian's going to show us how to make cocktails," Julie sends a wicked glance my way. "Did you think he was going to be a stripper, Alice?"

"No, I…" my face is red. "Maybe," I admit sheepishly.

"Sorry to disappoint you," Ian grins, and we follow him into the dining room, which Julie has set up with a wipe-clean table mat and places for all of us with our own cocktail shakers and glasses.

"I could kill you," I say to Julie. "But also, thanks!"

"No problem, my friend. My pleasure."

As the evening wears on, and we've all made and tested a huge range of cocktails – and mocktails, too, I begin to feel very tired, and a little bit sick. Time to stop drinking, I think. I thank Ian and stand with Julie to wave him off.

"You are the best," I say to my friend.

"I am, it's true!"

"Thanks for not getting me a stripper."

"Hey, the night's still young…"

I decide she's kidding and I head into the kitchen to put the kettle on. David and Sophie come in. David puts his arm around me.

"Alice," Sophie says, "I know it's your hen do, but would you mind very much if I head over to Amber's? I think I've maybe had enough here."

"You mean everyone's too old and drunk for you?"

She smiles.

"I'll give her a lift," says David. "I've only been on the mocktails and I promised Sam I'd buy him a pint, too. Besides, Martin's had enough as well. He's ready for his bed. I can take Sophie up to Amber's then Martin can have the car and get home to free the babysitter, while I have a few drinks with your husband-to-be."

"Sounds like a plan," I say. "Sam will be really chuffed to see you – and Sophie, that is absolutely fine, as long as you're back in time for lunch with your dad tomorrow."

"Of course."

"Alright, then. Seems like you've got it all covered."

"Bye, Mummy Number Two," Sophie grins.

"Hey! I don't think I want to be a number two."

"Alright then, I'll stick with Alice."

"Much better."

David hugs me. "Not long till you're Mrs Branvall now," he says. "It's been written in the stars forever, you know."

"Well, I don't know about that, but thank you. It sounds nice, doesn't it?"

"It sounds like a nice plump cook from a country kitchen," he says as he scoots away out of reach.

Mrs Branvall. It does sound a bit like that. But I like it.

Mum comes in soon after David and Sophie have left. She catches me sitting alone at the kitchen table.

"Are you alright, love?" she smiles.

"Yes, thanks. More than alright. Just a bit tired."

"You must be exhausted. But what a lovely night. I'm so proud of you, Alice."

"Thank you, Mum."

"And so happy you and Sam are getting married. I'd never have said anything, of course, but it's never felt quite right to me, you having Ben and not being married. It's old-fashioned, I know."

"It's strange, isn't it?" I put two mugs on the side and a teabag in each, pouring boiling water on top. "I'm not religious so it hasn't felt important to me in that way but in my mind I've always thought I would get married. Then I wasn't sure that Sam was too bothered, and it was more important to me that I was with the right man than that I was somebody's wife. But I'm so happy. I can't wait."

"Nor me. And your dad's beside himself! He was gutted he couldn't come to Sam's stag do."

"Ahh, poor Dad! Jim was staying out of it as well, though. I think Dad might feel a bit old if he was there."

"Your dad? Never. He's twenty-five in his mind, and he always will be."

"Yeah, that sounds about right."

I spoon out the teabags and pour in a little milk to each mug then hand one to Mum.

"Shall we take these outside?" I suggest. "I fancy a bit of fresh air."

"That sounds good. I'm a bit worried Julie's going to start drinking games soon. I am too old for drinking games."

"Me too! Come on, let's sneak into the garden."

I open the door expecting a bright, clear sky but we are greeted by a steady gentle rain.

"Oh," I say. "Maybe it's not such a good idea."

We shuffle back into the kitchen and sit at the table, the kitchen door closed but doing a poor job of muffling the shrieks of laughter from the lounge.

"Cheers, Mum," I say.

"Cheers, my favourite daughter. To happy times."

20

When Mum and I venture back from the kitchen, it is to a cacophony of cackling and belly laughs.

"God, I hope it doesn't wake Ben and Zinnia up," I say, feeling like the party-pooper I am. And this is meant to be my party! If truth be told, though, I'm ready for bed now. Still, I put my best smile on and head into the lounge, Mum following close behind.

We are greeted by the sight of Julie and Janie wrapped in toilet roll, with Karen assisting Janie and Sarah doubled over with laughter as she tries to pass a toilet roll between Julie's legs.

"I won't ask," I say, and they all look at me, and burst into more fits of laughter.

"You were meant to be involved in this!" Julie says reproachfully. "You're the blushing bride."

There is a snort of laughter from Janie, who looks more drunk than I have possibly ever seen her.

"I am," I say, "it's true." I gently pull the door closed behind me.

"Go on then," Karen throws a toilet roll to me. "We're making wedding dresses. Sue, you sort your daughter out. We need to send some photos to the boys."

"Sam can't see me in my dress before the wedding," I say, while Mum smiles at me apologetically as she begins to wind the toilet paper around my waist.

"Best dress wins a… shot of tequila!" calls Julie.

"Make it rubbish, Mum," I say, and she smiles quietly.

Just as Mum is winding the roll up and over my shoulders, doing one then the other – "You're getting too into this, Mum!" – I think I hear something. *Please don't let it be Ben*, I think. *Or Zinnia, for that matter*. I am not convinced Julie's in the best state to soothe a tired almost-toddler.

"Shhh!" I say, and Julie and Janie look at each other and laugh. What has got into Janie? She's normally quiet and calm. "I heard something," I say, gesturing to the stereo. "Can you turn that down please, Karen?"

Sam's mum pulls a mock-salute, to the amusement of my so-called friends, but she turns the music off.

Ding-dong.

There. I knew I'd heard something. But who's going to be at the door at this time of night? I hope it isn't the neighbours. I know we're being loud but I don't think we're being that bad.

"Could you go and answer it?" I ask Mum, wrapped as Julie and I are in Super Soft Value.

"OK."

I follow as best I can to the door of the room, thinking I don't really want Mum alone, answering the door to strangers, late at night.

Julie comes up behind me. "Are you having fun?"

"Yes," I say. "I really am. Thank you, Julie, for sorting this out. It's lovely."

"Well, we're a bit old and boring these days, aren't we? And I know, we have to be really but it doesn't hurt to remind ourselves that we can still be stupid and childish sometimes, does it?"

"No. You're absolutely right. I love it. And I love you. Hang on – this isn't actually a stripper, is it?"

"I wish! Hand on heart, it's not. I may forever regret not getting you one, though. I'd have loved to see your face!"

I hear Mum say "Hello" in a surprised tone, as though she knows the person she's greeting.

"Is Alice there?" I hear a tentative reply.

"Lydia!" I blurt out. I hope Janie didn't hear. I hurry to the door, as fast as my toilet-roll-wrapped legs will allow. Mum steps back.

"Alice!" Lydia says. She is covered by the porch but behind her steady drips of water fall quickly from the roof and glint in the light, as they kamikaze to the ground and begin their journey back to the sea, to start the process all over again.

"We're a bit, erm, busy," I say, lifting my arms helplessly and feeling guilty now that I hadn't invited her but, really, how could I have?

"I know. It's your hen do. I'm sorry to have interrupted."

How the heck does she know it's my hen do? I'll never get over how people seem to know everything that goes on in this town.

"But I didn't know where else to go. And I thought Janie must be here. It's… it's Jonathan, you see."

"Jonathan?" My mind works fast, to try and process what she's saying. Hoping against hope that Janie can't hear. But it's too late.

Looking like a cheap fancy-dress mummy, Janie appears in the hallway behind me. The drunken smile is gone, and her face is set and hard. "What about Jonathan?"

Lydia starts to cry.

"What is it, Lydia?" I ask.

"Yes, come on," Julie's voice has taken on an edge. "Don't just stand there crying. Spit it out."

"He's gone."

"Gone? Gone where?" I ask.

"I don't know."

"Come in," I say impatiently, wanting to close the door and shut the rest of the world out from whatever mess is about to be revealed. "Now what do you mean you don't know?"

"I… he… I pissed him off."

"Right."

"What were you doing with him, to piss him off?" Janie's voice is cold.

"It's not what you think," Lydia turns to Janie. "Or not how it sounds. It's… I knew, that you'd be here. As it's Alice's hen do."

I wonder again how she could possibly have known that, but I don't think it's the pressing point here.

"And I went up to Amethi," Lydia says sheepishly. "I wanted to see him. But not like that. I know he loves you, Janie. And I know things aren't great between you but I'm not trying to make them worse, I promise."

"You know nothing," Janie hisses.

I feel like I shouldn't be here and Mum has already made herself scarce, retreating into the lounge and the safety of Karen and Sarah. Julie and I stand back, ready to intervene if we need to, as Janie moves towards Lydia.

"I've been trying to poach him." Lydia looks at me now.

"Poach?" Janie asks. "Is that what you call it?"

"I mean for work," Lydia says quickly.

"What?" Julie and I exclaim as one.

"Felicity asked me to," she says, like a child.

And if Felicity asked you to jump off a bridge, would you do that? I want to ask, but my mind has caught up now and I've latched on to the most pressing point.

"OK. We'll talk about that in a bit. The important thing now is what do you mean that Jon's gone?"

"He… I gave him a lift to town. He wanted to go and

see Sam after he'd finished work, buy him a drink. So I dropped him off, near the Mainbrace, and I went back to the Bay. But I was upset we'd fallen out, and I went down to the pub to find him. Only... Sam and Luke said he never turned up."

"OK," I say, thinking this sounds like a bit of an over-reaction, to say he's 'gone'. Having said that, I do have a rumbling feeling of anxiety in my abdomen. "I still don't know why you think something's wrong, though. He must have just headed home, I expect."

"I rang him, and he didn't answer."

"That still doesn't mean he's *gone* anywhere," I object. "If you'd fallen out, he probably didn't want to talk to you." I could have minced my words, I suppose, but I can sense Julie's intense irritation with Lydia and I can't say I'm feeling too fond of her right now, either.

"No, but I saw Bea's brother, David, going into the Mainbrace. He said he'd just walked Martin to the Island car park, and they'd seen Jon walking out of town."

I still don't get it.

"Oh no," Janie says.

Lydia looks at her properly for the first time. It's like they both know something. And Janie's face is white.

"What?" I say.

"He's done this before," Janie says.

"Done what?" I almost shout, incredibly anxious now.

"Gone up on the cliffs."

"At night-time? He wouldn't do that."

"He would. And he did. Just the other night."

"What? When?"

"When I was at Mum's," Janie says. "When he asked you to fill in for him," she looks to Julie.

"Oh."

"Why?"

"Because… I don't know. He says he was just walking, but I didn't like it. He tried to call me when he was up there but I didn't answer. I was too annoyed with him," says Janie. "I… I don't know what's happened to him lately. Sometimes I feel like I hardly know him."

"Come on," I say, "let's go and sit in the kitchen and work out exactly what's going on here. Julie, would you mind telling the others that the party's over?"

"Of course not."

Suddenly our toilet roll wrappings seem very inappropriate. I pull at mine, scrunching it up and dumping it on the side in the kitchen. Janie does the same with hers and by the time she gets back, having seen Mum, Sarah and Karen out, Julie's already unravelled and disposed of hers.

"Right," I say. "I do want to know what's going on but, most importantly, we need to find out where Jon is. Are you saying he's gone off on the cliffs tonight?" I ask Lydia.

"I… I don't know but he's not answering his phone and that's where David says he seemed to be heading."

Janie has her own phone to her ear, dialling and re-dialling Jon's number. I hear the sound of Jon's voicemail message.

"Right," says Julie. "Well, we need to find out where he is. Maybe he's walking back to Amethi."

"In this weather?" I ask, eyeing Lydia's soaking hair and shoulders.

"Could be," Julie shrugs. "People do strange things when they're pissed off. Or maybe he's got a taxi home."

"Hang on," Janie says, then looks shame-faced. "I can track him. His phone, I mean. I… turned the location setting on."

"Without him knowing?" I am shocked.

"Yes. He's been acting so strangely lately. And I knew you were sniffing around," she says to Lydia.

"I have not been *sniffing around*," says Lydia in disgust.

"Lydia, why don't you go and get some of my clean dry clothes, and dry your hair?" Julie suggests. "Come on, I'll show you where my room is."

I smile gratefully at my friend. It's amazing how fast people sober up when they need to.

"OK," I say to Janie. "Now you can tell me exactly what's been going on. I know Jonathan's not been happy. Nor you. But we need to sort this out, and we need to find him. If Lydia's right – and it is *if* – we need to make sure he's safe. The coastal path is not a good place to be at night, especially in this weather."

As Janie opens the location tracker on her phone, she talks. "It's true, he went off the other day. He did say he was just walking, but he also left me a weird message."

"What kind of weird message?"

"He was crying," she says now, with a sob of her own. "But I didn't listen to the message till the next day, when he was back home. And I went straight to him. I've been so wrapped up in myself, and in not feeling very happy here, I've not been paying enough attention to him."

"Don't blame yourself," I say. "I don't suppose Lydia coming back on the scene has been particularly helpful, either. And Jon not telling you about it."

"No, but I do know now that there is nothing going on there. I mean, *she* might want it to be different," she says scornfully, her eyes on her phone screen. "There's no sign of him. The last location was somewhere in town. I bet he's turned his phone off."

"Keep looking," I say, pulling my own phone from my

pocket, "maybe it's just connecting. I'll call Sam and see if he's seen Jon. Maybe he'll have gone back to the pub."

It takes three attempts to get Sam to answer.

"Hello my beloved betrothed," he slurs.

"Sam?"

"Yes, my love?" There are loud, familiar male voices and a gale of laughter.

"Is Jon there?"

"No. He's not." Sam's voice has taken on a less jubilant tone.

"Has he been with you at all?"

"No. He hasn't."

"What's wrong?"

"Hang on…" There is much rustling down the phone line and I hear a muffled Sam's voice saying, "'Scuse me, mate," more than once. Then the quieter sound of, presumably, the outside world.

"Sam?" I say.

"Yep." He sounds a little pissed off.

"Have you seen Jon or not?"

"I've seen him," he says, slurring slightly again.

"Where?"

"Earlier on," he says, "out here."

I presume he means outside the pub.

"OK, and was he alright?"

"Dunno. Well, not after I had a word with him."

"What do you mean, a word?"

"He…" Sam sighs, and I am almost certain he's sitting down. I imagine him pinching the bridge of his nose between his thumb and forefinger. "Is Janie there?" he asks.

"Yes." I can't let this drag on. "Lydia turned up here, Sam. She said Jon's gone missing or something."

"Did she now?"

"Yes, I'll explain it all in a bit. It's not how it sounds. Janie's here and she knows all about it. Look, I'll put you on speakerphone."

"Sam?" Janie says, and she seems very young all of a sudden. "Have you seen Jonathan?"

"Yeah, I did see him. He was… you say Lydia's there?"

"Yes," Janie says impatiently. "She is. Don't worry about it. There's nothing going on between them."

"But I saw him getting out of her car."

"Yes, we know all about that," Janie waves her hand dismissively, as if Sam can see. "She wants him to work at the Bay. But he's not interested. She was giving him a lift into town so he could have a drink with you."

"Oh. Shit."

"What?" Janie asks, a note of panic high in her voice.

"I may have told him to fuck off."

"*What?*" she asks again, in a shriek this time.

"I didn't know," he protests. "I thought he was. You know…"

"Seeing Lydia?" I suggest helpfully.

"Yeah."

"No, he's not, Sam," I say, my concern for Jonathan making me sound more angry than I really feel.

"Well how was I supposed to know that?"

"You weren't," I admit. "Sorry. It's just that Lydia said he's gone off up on the cliffs. Said David saw him. Is David there?"

"Yeah, he's… a bit pissed. He didn't say anything about seeing Jonathan. Or Lydia."

"No, he probably didn't want to ruin your night," I say, looking at Janie, who is frantically refreshing her screen. "Look, we're trying to work out where Jon is. Don't worry, I'm sure it's nothing. I'll let you know in a bit."

"Right. I hope he's OK."

"I'm sure he will be," I say, as much for Janie's sake as Sam's.

"Let me know when you find him."

"I will. Love you, Sam."

"I love you, too."

I can't help thinking, selfishly, that this was meant to be *our* night – mine and Sam's – that we should be enjoying ourselves with our friends right now. Yet here we are, embroiled in drama, and not of our own making. I'm so tired and my head's hurting and all I want is to be tucked up in bed, with Sam's arms around me.

"No good?" I ask Janie.

She shakes her head.

"OK... we need to think this through. I think we need to speak to Ron."

"Ron?"

"Yes. We need to find Jon, but it's not a good idea for us to go off into the dark on that slippery path, in the rain."

"You think we need to call Search and Rescue?" Janie's face is paler than ever.

"I don't know. That's what I want to ask Ron."

"I'll do it," she says. She picks up her phone and waits for a moment. "Hi, Mum. Are you home yet? ... Yes, I'm fine ... Not, it's nothing like that. Listen," she interjects strongly, between what I can only assume are bouts of Karen interrogating her about Lydia. "Jon's missing, maybe up on the coastal path. I need to speak to Ron. Is he awake? ... Could you wake him? Please?"

Janie looks at me while she waits then I hear the distinct sound of Ron's voice. "You OK, Janie, love?"

"Yes, well, no. I... don't know where Jon is. There's a chance he's up walking the path, on the cliffs. I can't get

159

hold of him … No, we don't know for sure, but he was seen going that way and, well, I know he was up there the other night. When I was staying over. He's… been a bit down."

Oh, Jonathan, I think. I knew he wasn't happy but now it seems he may have been even more unhappy than I'd realised.

"Could I have the phone, please?" I ask Janie and she seems grateful to hand it over.

"Hi, Ron. It's Alice. Look, it's a bit of a weird one, because we don't know for sure where Jonathan is. But he's not answering his phone, and his last known location was town – David saw him, and he was heading in the direction of the cliffs."

"Which side of town?"

"Up west, I think." My mind flits briefly to the little shepherd's hut up there, where Sam and I once sheltered from a storm. Maybe Jon's there now, in the dark. It would be cold and damp but at least he'd be safe.

"OK. But you don't know for sure?"

"No. I can check with David, though. We just don't know what to do, whether to call Search and Rescue, or if we're being overdramatic and just need to keep calling him until he hopefully switches his phone back on."

"I think from what you're telling me, Alice, you can't take any chances. Has he a history of depression?"

"God… yes. I've only realised it recently but yes. And he has been quite down lately." I look at Janie and she nods.

"Has he been drinking?"

"I don't think so. He'd been working and had got a lift into town. I don't think he'd have had a chance to be drinking."

If only Sam hadn't had a go at him, Jonathan could be in the pub now. But Sam wasn't to know. He was just trying to protect his sister.

"OK. Well, I think we need to call it in."

"But what if he's not up there?"

"Better safe than sorry, Alice," Ron says. "I'll sort it. I'd better go."

"OK. Thank you, Ron." As we end the call, I feel cold. Suddenly, it feels real. Jonathan could be out there. Injured, or worse.

"It'll be OK, Janie," I put my arm round her. "This is just a precaution. And lucky us, knowing Ron. He can keep us informed." I don't know if this is true, actually. He'll be more bothered about doing his job, if the lifeboat is involved with this. He's a proper, real-life hero. Karen's definitely landed on her feet. "Look, I'm just going to text Sam, to let him know what's going on. Then I'll put the kettle on and hopefully we'll hear something soon."

Presently, Julie and Lydia come back into the kitchen. "I'm going to get a taxi to take Lydia back to the Bay," Julie says, looking hard at Lydia.

"OK. I'm sure it will be fine," I say to Lydia, who is close to tears. There's no point in making her feel worse than she already does. It seems to me there's been enough bad feeling lately.

Janie's phone pings. "It's Ron. He says they're sending out search teams on foot, and the inshore lifeboat."

"Shit." It's weird. It doesn't make the situation any worse – if anything, it makes it better – but knowing that this is being treated as an emergency makes it feel much more real.

"What if something's happened to him, Alice? What if he's… done something to himself?"

"That won't have happened," I say firmly, knowing full well that I can't promise anything. I'm thinking of stories where people have seemed absolutely fine then left their home one morning and never come back – whether they've run away, or ended their lives, either way they've felt unable to go on with things as they are. I am thinking of Geoff, my ex-boyfriend, who time and distance have taught me was a very troubled soul. But Jon's not that unhappy, I tell myself, though I know it's not that simple.

I see Jon's face. That first time I met him, at the Sail Loft. Good-looking, young and confident. That's how he seemed then. The looks – no denying, he's incredibly attractive, though I've known him so long I barely notice this anymore. Young – he was then; and he is now, in the great scheme of things. Confident, though – now I doubt this. Was he ever confident in the way I'd thought? Was his messing about and philandering a sign of insecurity rather than arrogance?

Now, I see him as Meg and I found him the other day. Knees drawn to his chest, leaning into them, amidst the earth, at the base of a tree.

I sigh, without meaning to.

"You're worried about him, aren't you?" Lydia asks.

"Of course she is," Julie snaps. *And no thanks to you* – this goes unsaid but we all know that's what she means.

"It's nobody's fault," I say. "Not yours, Lydia; not yours, Janie – and not Jonathan's, either."

"I've ruined your hen night," Lydia sobs.

"Oh my god, Lydia, as if that's important."

I shoot Julie a warning look. I'm not happy with Lydia, either, but it's plain how bad she feels. And yes, she's acted stupidly, with only her own interests at heart, but it's not a far cry from Julie's own behaviour that time when we were freshly returned to Cornwall. She messed Luke about; and Gabe, who she had been engaged to and dumped by letter.

We all do stupid things sometimes.

We jump at the sound of a car horn outside.

"The taxi," Julie says.

"Of course."

Lydia quietly gathers her wet things. "I'm sorry," she says, quietly, to nobody in particular.

"It'll be OK," I say. "We'll let you know when there's news."

"I don't think I'll be able to sleep tonight."

Julie huffs. I just stand and see Lydia out. "I'll be in touch." It sounds like the end of a job interview.

Julie, Janie and I go into the lounge.

"I'm going to light a fire," Julie says. "I don't know why. It's the middle of summer. We'll probably overheat."

"No, it's a nice idea," I say. The idea of something warm to focus on is appealing. Comforting. The constant rain is lending a dampness to the air.

Janie tries Jon's phone every five minutes but it's always the same. Straight to voicemail.

I check my own phone, not really expecting to have heard from Jon if Janie hasn't, but also hoping to have heard from Sam. I don't want him to feel bad, especially when he's only just started to feel better about things. There are no new messages, and I can't believe it's only 10.57pm. It feels like the middle of the night.

Julie lights the fire and makes a cafetiere of coffee. She brings it in on a tray, with three large mugs, a jug of warm milk, and a tray of brownies.

How is it that Ben and Zinnia have slept through all this? I hope that by the time they wake, even if none of us have slept a wink, this is all over and Jonathan is safe and well. I hope, in fact, that this is all a mistake and he was just making his way home when David and Martin saw him. It's possible, I tell myself. Phone signal is patchy on those quiet winding roads. That would explain why we can't get hold of him.

We drink the coffee and keep coming up with reassuring explanations of what has happened.

"Any word from Ron yet?" Julie asks, as if Janie or I wouldn't have mentioned it.

"No, not yet," I say as a message pings onto both my phone and Janie's at the same time. "Speak of the devil."

Nothing yet, girls. Take heart, he may not be out there at all. I'm down at the station so I'll keep an eye on everything. It will be OK.

"Good old Ron," Julie says warmly.

"Yeah," I say, grateful for his words. I think of the crew on the boat, and the people searching the cliffs. It can't be safe for them, surely? I feel awful. What if Jon's not even out there and they're risking their lives?

There's a key in the front door and we all look at each other.

"Hello?" comes Luke's tentative voice, trying to keep the sound down.

"We're in here," says Julie, standing to kiss him as he enters the room.

"Everyone alright?" he asks. "Janie? Alice?"

"Yeah, well, kind of. Where's Sam?" I ask, peering over his shoulder.

"He's gone down the lifeboat station, see if he can help. He felt bad, about Jon." He looks at Janie.

"We all feel bad about Jon," she says glumly. "If only he'd turn up now. Ring on the doorbell. I just want to put my arms around him."

"And you will," says Luke. "This'll be something and nothing, you'll see."

He pours himself a coffee and takes a huge bite of a brownie; they've lain untouched until now, none of the three of us feeling the slightest bit hungry.

"Was it a good night?" I ask hopefully, feeling the futility of the words.

"Yeah, it was," Luke says, "until…"

"I could kill Lydia," Julie says.

"It's not her fault," I say. "It's just…"

"A mess," Janie supplies. "Just a big mess."

"Has Jon done anything like this before?" Luke asks Janie. I'm impressed by his directness.

"Well, I told Alice and Julie, he did go off the other night – but I was staying at Mum's. I had no idea, until I got back the next day."

"And he'd… what? Gone for a wander?"

"Yes, I guess," she smiles unconvincingly. "He'd wanted to think, he said."

"OK, well that sounds pretty normal."

"Yeah, but. It's hard to explain. It was more than that. We've been having problems. Neither of us has been happy, really, but it's not his fault. I've been a bit wrapped up in how fed up I am in Cornwall. Sorry," she says, "I know you all love it here. Jon thinks it's his fault, but it's not. It's just – this isn't my home in the same way it's Sam's. I haven't lived here since I was eight. My home's in Spain. I miss it there. But I love being close to Sam, and you, Alice. And I do love Jonathan."

"But he's not always easy to live with?" I suggest.

"Well… no. He's not. He gets down, sometimes. Never angry, or nasty. Just very… low. I suppose I've been quite dependent on him, which probably hasn't helped. And I over-reacted about the Lydia thing because I'm pissed off anyway. Maybe I resent him, a bit, because being with him

165

means being away from Spain. And when I found out he'd been keeping in touch with Lydia, I was angrier still. I thought he was making a fool of me and that I was living a life I'm not 100% happy with, to be with him while he was thinking about getting back together with his ex."

"But he wasn't…" I say.

"No, I know that now."

"So what set him off tonight?" asks Luke.

"I don't know, for sure. We've been talking a lot this week, about the future. And I know he's stressed about work and not making it in the way he'd always imagined. God, maybe he should take Lydia's offer to be at the Bay. Maybe he can make it a signature restaurant. Sorry…" she trails off, realising that's not exactly what Julie and I want to hear.

"That's OK," I smile. "He should do his own thing. I think he needs to. But is it getting to him that much?"

"No, it's not just that. But it's like things gnaw away at him. Almost like he wants them to. He's punishing himself for making me unhappy, and hates himself for not coming clean with me about Lydia. And he sees other people – you two, and you and Sam, with your families and what he sees as perfect lives. He thinks he can't do it, and it won't happen for him."

We are all quiet.

"Poor Jon," I say.

"Yes. And poor Janie, too," says Julie. "You're not having much fun."

"It doesn't matter," says Janie. "God, I'd never go back to Spain again if only Jon was OK. I need to make more effort here. Not be so wrapped up in what I'm missing."

"Maybe," I say. "But you are entitled to your own opinions, you know."

Our phones ping again. Janie is quicker than me.

"Oh god," she says.

"What?" I look at my screen.

No need to panic but the inshore boat have spotted what looks like a person on the rocks, out near the giant's cave. Not confirmed. I'll keep you informed.

"Shit," I say. I pass the phone to Julie.

"Shit," she confirms.

The doorbell rings, startling the four of us. I put my hand on Janie's shoulder. "That'll be Sam. Bet he's lost his key. Don't worry, about Jon. That could be anyone… or it might not even be a person. Ron says it's not confirmed. They'll need to get close enough to see. Sam'll be able to tell us more, he's quite the expert now. I'll go and let him in."

The rain is bouncing off the window on the front door and I can just make out Sam's shape in the light from the hallway.

"Lost your key, have you? Julie'll have your guts for gart…" I open the door but it's not Sam at all. "Jonathan!" I gasp, and I throw my arms around his soaking shoulders. I don't know if I've ever been so happy to see anyone.

"Janie! It's Jon!" I call and as she dashes into the hallway I stand back so she can throw herself at him.

Julie and Luke come through too and the air is filled with the laughter of relief.

"I'd better tell Ron," I say, and head back into the lounge to get my phone.

But if it's not Jonathan on the rocks, I think, who is it?

21

We usher the soaking Jonathan in and Luke sends him and Janie through to his bedroom, to rifle through his clothes for something dry to wear. Jon is shivering and pale. With the terrible weather outside, it feels like autumn, rather than midsummer. Especially with the vague smell of woodsmoke drifting through from the lounge.

"I'd better phone Ron," I say to nobody in particular and I go into the lounge to pick up my phone. I wander across to the window, which is being lashed with rain, the trees angrily throwing their branches back and forth, casting moving shadows onto the living room wall. I look at the mesmerising flames of the fire, hypnotic behind the window of the stove.

Ron doesn't answer straightaway and I'm just about to hang up when I hear his voice. "Alice?" he sounds brisk and efficient.

"He's here," I exclaim, and with those words an immense relief floods through me. "Jonathan's here!"

"He's…" It takes Ron a few moments to compute what I've just said. "Well, that is great news, Alice. Really great."

"Yes. I'm so sorry to have put you all through this, unnecessarily."

"You haven't put us through anything, Alice. And in fact, it's possible this has led us to somebody else who is in trouble. Because the inshore crew have confirmed there is definitely somebody down on the rocks. I can't tell you any more right now and I'd better go but I am so very pleased it's not Jonathan out there. Is he OK?"

"I think so. Janie's with him. I'll send you a text in a bit to let you know. I don't want to disturb you again. I hope that other person's alright."

"Me too, Alice. They've got the best crew in Cornwall out for them, though."

"That's good to know." I smile at Ron's loyalty even in these pressing circumstances. I can just imagine Sam being like that one day. And I get it now, a little more; Sam's passion for the lifeboat and his wanting to be part of something like this. If that had been Jon, there would be people out there potentially putting themselves at risk to rescue him. And those people are there trying to help somebody else, right now. I can see why Sam wants to be part of that and I know it's selfish of me to want him to change his mind.

"Sam got back to you OK as well, did he?" There is a slight note of amusement in Ron's voice.

"Sam? No, he's not back yet. Why, have you seen him?"

"Oh yeah, I've seen him alright. Three sheets to the wind, he was. Wanted to help with the search but I told him he'd be as much use as a chocolate teapot. Sent him home to you instead. Anyways, I really had better be going."

"When was this, Ron?" I am suddenly breathless, like the wind's been knocked out of me.

"Oh, I couldn't really say. I've had my mind on the search really. I s'pose it could've been a good hour back. Look, I've got to go. It sounds like they're getting the helicopter out."

"Of course," I say weakly. "Bye, Ron."

I take a long, deep breath. Let it out very, very slowly.

"Luke?" I call.

"Yeah?" he pokes his head around the door.

"When you left the pub, was Sam with you?"

"Nah, he'd gone off on a mission. Said he was going to the lifeboat station, see if he could help. Proper superhero, your bloke!"

"I just spoke to Ron and he said Sam's not there."

"Really? That's weird."

"He sent him away, he said – Sam was too pissed to be any use."

"Ha, yeah that doesn't surprise me."

"But it was about an hour ago. Maybe longer."

"OK. So he should be back soon."

"He should have been back ages ago!" I exclaim. That relief, at Jonathan's safe return, has been replaced by a deep, dark dread at the pit of my stomach. I know Sam, you see. I know how his mind works. And how he'll have felt about Jonathan going missing. Especially if he felt responsible for it.

Luke catches up with me. "You don't think…?"

"I don't know." But I do. I think I do.

I try Sam's number. It rings and rings. There is no answer.

"Let me try," says Luke, to the same effect. "OK, OK," he says, sitting down heavily and resting his head in his hands. "Try not to panic," like he's saying this to himself as much as for my benefit. "He could just be being sick in an alley somewhere," he says hopefully. "He was pretty pissed."

There are not many situations when the thought of Sam throwing up in a dark street would be comforting but that possibility is a million times more positive than the other one.

"Or he could have gone back to the pub?" I say hopefully, though I'm not convinced, and neither is Luke.

"The party was kind of breaking up," he says. "With Jon missing and all. It didn't seem right to carry on drinking.

170

Besides, we're all old boys now, aren't we? Need our beds."

"What's up?" Julie asks as she comes in. "I thought we'd be celebrating."

Luke and I both look at her.

"What is it?" she asks, alarmed.

"It's Sam," I say. "We don't know where he is."

"Still at the pub?"

"No, I don't think so. He went to see if he could help at the lifeboat station. Ron sent him packing."

"I think…" I can hardly bear to say the words. To do so would make the possibility all the more real. "I think that could be him, out there."

"Nooooo."

"Think about it," I say. "He wanted to help. He thought it was his fault that Jon went off – or partly his fault, anyway. The last thing he said to Jon was to tell him to fuck off. It would be just like Sam to go haring off to try and fix things."

"Have you phoned him?"

"Of course!" I say.

"Sorry, stupid thing to ask. And no answer?"

"No, it's just ringing out."

"OK. Has he got location tracking turned on?"

I think of Janie tracking Jonathan. This idea has never occurred to me, with Sam. I've never felt any need to doubt him. But now I realise it's not all about that. It's about safety.

"Log onto Google as Sam, if you can," Julie says, suddenly sensible and practical.

"Yes!" says Luke. "Great idea. If he's got it turned on, we might be able to see where he is."

"What's going on?" asks Janie, from the doorway. Jonathan stands sheepishly behind her.

"Janie," I say, not wishing to break the news it may be her brother out there; just when she's got her boyfriend back safe and sound.

"It's Sam," says Julie, never one to beat around the bush. "It's possible that it's him out there."

"What? How could it be?" Janie asks, moving into the room and looking panicked.

Jon steps forward. "Please don't say he's looking for me."

"We don't know," I say, feeling a little stronger now. I don't want Jonathan thinking this is his fault. "We're not sure. I'm just going to try and log on to his laptop, see if Google can tell us where he is.

"Oh god," says Jon, "please tell me it's not him."

My hands are shaking as I pull Sam's computer from its case and onto my knees. I open it up and type in his password. Then I log into Google. "What now?"

Luke takes the computer from me and taps away at the keyboard, his face intent on the screen. I see him frown. His mouth opens but no words come out.

"It's him, isn't it?" I ask. "He's out there on the cliffs."

Luke hands the computer to me. I can see a map, zoomed in to the area of green that denotes the wild area where the coastal path skirts up and away from the town. There is a little blue pointer here. I look at Luke. His face says it all.

I zoom out a bit and I can see Sam's movements from today, marked in blue. From here to Jim's house. From there to town. Between the various pubs, to the Mainbrace, to the lifeboat station. To the coastal path. And there the trail ends.

"Phone Ron," Luke says.

There is no answer. I imagine Ron rolling his eyes, not willing to be distracted any further by me. I text instead:

Ron. It might be Sam out there. He's not come home and Google shows his phone is out on the coastal path. Have you found him? Please call when you can.

It takes less than a minute for Ron to call back. "Alice? Is it Sam? Are you sure? They've winched up the casualty–" *Casualty?* My heart is thumping, "–and haven't id'd him yet."

"You mean, he's…"

"Whoever it is, Alice, is alive, but unconscious. They're being taken to Plymouth. Got some nasty injuries by the sound of things. Is it Sam? Are you sure?" he asks again.

"No, I'm not sure, Ron, but it looks like he went that way. Maybe to look for Jonathan," I cast a look Jon's way. He is sitting with Janie, both of them pale-faced and holding hands. Sod it. I need to tell Ron what I know. "He had a falling out with Jon, over a misunderstanding. I think when Sam realised Jonathan might have been in trouble and that he couldn't help you out, he might have taken it on himself to go and look for Jon himself."

"Oh god. I sent him away," Ron says.

"You had to. You couldn't have a drunk trainee hanging around the station." Whatever the situation, it is not Ron's fault, and neither is it Jon's.

"What am I going to tell Karen?" he asks.

"I don't know," I say. I am not sure where this strength has come from but I do know that sitting round feeling sorry for ourselves is not going to help Sam, if it is him. I end the call and tell the others what's going on.

"I'm going out to look for him," Luke says.

"I'll come too," Jonathan stands.

"No, mate, you've only just got dry," Luke says gently.

My god, he's such a kind person. I sneak a glance at Julie whose eyes rest on her husband, full of love.

"I'll come with you," she says.

"But it's dark and rainy," I protest.

"We'll be alright. We'll go prepared. And we won't do anything silly. But if Sam's phone's out there, he might be with it. He might be sheltering in that shepherd's hut you and him seem so keen on–" he chances a cheeky grin, "– he might have just fallen asleep up there. He can't take his drink these days, that lad."

"I hope so," I say. "OK. You two go but don't take any silly risks. I'll stay here in case Sam gets back, and to keep an eye on the kids. Janie, Jon, what are you going to do? You need to get some rest."

"We're not going anywhere, Alice," says Jonathan. "Not till we know Sam's OK."

Janie nods her agreement. I'm sorry she's going through this, and I am so glad that Sophie went up to Amber's. Meanwhile, Ben and Zinnia sleep sweetly on, with no idea of all the drama taking place within their home.

When Luke and Julie have gone, with promises between us to call as soon as there is any news, I sneak into Zinnia's room and check that all is well. She is on her back, arms bent upwards, legs bent out, like an upside-down frog.
I tiptoe out and go into Ben's room. He is curled on his side, his tiger toy tucked under his arm. I kiss his soft cheek and listen to him breathing. I try to calm my own breath. Pull myself together before I go back into the lounge. I am glad Jonathan and Janie are there but at the same time I want to be alone. When I do go back in, they are talking. They look up at me.

"Alice," says Jonathan. "I am so sorry for all the trouble I've caused."

"Jon, you have not caused any trouble. Well, maybe a bit. You've been having a tough time."

His eyes glisten with tears.

"I mean it," I say. "I didn't realise quite how tough a time until tonight."

"No," he says. "It just comes rushing in at me sometimes. But I didn't mean to worry you all, you know. I wasn't planning anything... dramatic. I just needed to walk and the wind and the rain seemed like they'd help wash it all away. I feel like banging my head on a rock sometimes, to make the darkness go away, but I've never felt like actually banging my head on a rock to... I've never felt like... harming myself. I just know I'm no good until I've got myself back together again. Walking makes me feel like me again. And it gives me some space to let my thoughts run their course. But I promise – I *promise* – I didn't mean to hurt myself. Janie," he turns to her now, "I know I've been a miserable bastard lately. I don't know why. I have so much I love in my life, including you, and yet somehow it still isn't enough to keep the darkness at bay."

I look away while Janie puts her arms around him and he sobs into her neck. "I thought I'd lost you," she says.

I might have lost Sam, I think, *and you might have lost your brother*. But I don't say anything. No point thinking like that, but I think of that little boy I've just been in to see. How he could wake up in the morning to a new day, and a new life, without his dad. And Sophie. How can I tell her, if anything's happened to Sam?

We sit quietly for a while. Tense and waiting for news. I can't keep my eyes off my phone. When finally it rings, I see immediately it's Julie.

"Alice?" she says. "We've found Sam's phone."

But not Sam, I think immediately. I know.

"It was lit up, the torch was switched on. It was… near the edge of the path. And there are–" she chokes slightly on her words, "–it looks like somebody's slipped in the mud nearby, at the edge of the path. By the rocks."

"I'll phone Ron."

From thereon in, everything is a blur.

Ron is evidently upset but he keeps a cool, calm head. "The helicopter's due to arrive at Plymouth any minute now. Casualty on board in a serious but stable condition."

"Has he gained consciousness yet?"

"No, I don't think so."

"So you still don't know who he is?"

"No."

I ring Julie back. "I have to go to Plymouth," I say. "In case it's Sam." Why do I say 'in case'? I know.

"Of course. We're on our way back, right now. We'll take care of things here. But you can't drive, Alice. You've been drinking."

"Shit." My mind flicks through the different options available. I hang up and dial another number.

"Dad?"

"Alice? Is everything OK?" He sounds sleepy, and is speaking in hushed tones.

"I…" suddenly the tears come. I am a daughter again; I can leave my own sense of responsibility to one side for a moment.

"What is it?"

"It's Sam. Or, I think it is. I need to get to Plymouth, to the hospital. Can you take me?"

"I can, I can, of course I can. But what's happened?"

"I don't know. I don't even know if it is Sam, not definitely, but I need to go."

"Tell him I'll do the Sail Loft breakfasts," Jon says and I look at him. He's pleased to be able to do something practical, I think.

"Thank you," I mouth, and relay the message to Dad.

"I'll be right there," Dad says.

Dad arrives at about the same time Julie and Luke get back home.

"I'll ring you," I tell Julie, as she hands me Sam's phone. "Give Ben a hug from me, will you? In the morning? Tell him I'll be back as soon as I can."

"Of course," she says. "And you never know, Sam might still turn up back here, with no idea of all the trouble he's caused!" She smiles and pulls me into a tight hug. "Whatever happens, I'm here for you, Griffiths. Always."

I have to pull away. I can't cry now. This is a time for action.

"Thank you, Julie. You're the best."

"I know," she chances a small smile.

And we are off, into the night, Dad and me.

I think of the time Paul came to my aid, when Mum was in hospital. The intense journey, speeding up the A30 and then the M5, with no idea of what I might find when I reached the hospital. This journey, by contrast, is so much shorter, but in the deep dark night, the weather still throwing its weight around and the windscreen wipers going ten to the dozen, it seems to go on forever. Dad has Radio 4 on, at a low volume; I can barely make out the words, but the soft, deep tones of the presenter offer a gentle comfort and the two of us barely speak. There is nothing much that either of us can say, and we both know that.

177

My phone pings sporadically.

Ron: **I am home with Karen. She wants to come to the hospital too. We'll see you there. News is that they're having to operate. I don't know any more details right now.**

Oh my god. My mind goes to eighteen-year-old Sam; he'd been in a road traffic accident not long after I'd gone back to the Midlands. I never knew, till ten years later. *He got through that*, I think. *He can get through this.* I'm done with thinking it might not be him who they rescued from the rocks. I am sure that it is.

Karen: **We are on our way. Janie is with us. See you soon Alice. Let me know when you get there xx**

Julie: **No news here but don't they say no news is good news? Jon is asleep on the settee. He's exhausted. Luke and I are sitting up. Kids still fast asleep. Let me know when you get there xxx**

I assure both Karen and Julie that I will let them know when we arrive but in reality I will be too busy trying to find Sam to think of texting or phoning. I will find out what's going on and then I'll let them know.

The sky is already lightening by the time we reach the hospital. The car park is reassuringly empty.

"Wouldn't be like this in the daytime," Dad says, pulling into a space.

I am already unbuckling my seatbelt and getting out of the car.

"I wonder what we do about paying for parking," Dad muses, then realises what he's saying. "Sorry, Alice. As if that matters. Come on, let's go and find Sam."

He's faster than me, Dad, and we rush towards the main building. The automatic doors open onto an empty space.

"Where should we go?" I ask, my wet trainers squeaking on the pristine floor. I spot a porter, disappearing past the end of the corridor.

"Excuse me!" I call, and he backs up, reappearing. "I'm looking for my fiancé. He's been brought in, I think, by helicopter."

The man comes towards us and gives us directions to the emergency department. When we're there, a nurse takes charge, as we explain the situation. "If he's in surgery," she tells us, "there's not a lot we can do right now but wait. There's a family-and-friends waiting area, and you can get a coffee there. I'll see what I can find out."

Dad and I sit, side-by-side, on the squeaky, wipe-clean seats in the waiting area. The coffee is hot and scalds my mouth but it's not altogether unpleasant. It makes me feel alive. Every now and then, I experience a wave of nausea.

"I think I need to eat something," I tell Dad, and press coins into the vending machine, getting us each a Picnic bar. At half-three in the morning, it wouldn't normally be my first choice, but it seems like it will fill me up, and give me some energy. I feel so tired but I couldn't go to sleep now even if I wanted to.

The nurse comes back. "I have some news," she says, "and it's good and bad."

Oh god.

"The patient did regain consciousness sporadically during the journey and gave his name as Sam. A card was found on his person, with the name Branvall."

Dad and I look at each other.

"Yes, that's him," I say, standing up.

"The bad news is I'm afraid you can't go and see him just yet," she says and the 'just yet' gives me a small glimmer of hope. "But you can soon. And I can tell you more now that we know for sure who it is. I'm afraid he… Sam… suffered some nasty injuries on his way down the cliff and they've had to do some fairly dramatic work on his right leg. It was a nasty break and the team have had to realign the bone and fix it in place with a plate and rods. He had to have general anaesthetic and will be under for a little while yet. When he wakes up, he's going to be confused and in a lot of pain, but the surgical team are pleased with how the operation's gone. He'll need to be on painkillers for some time, and the leg will be put in plaster. I hope to be able to let you see him soon."

"Oh my god, oh my god," I say. "I must tell Karen."

I reach for my phone.

"Alice?"

"It's him," I say, "and he's OK. I think. He hurt himself badly… falling down the cliff." As I say those words and the reality of what happened to Sam hits me properly, I find a lump in my throat and I can't say anymore.

Dad takes the phone from me, putting his spare arm round my shoulder and pulling me to him. "Karen? It's Phil. Yes, he's OK. The nurse said he's broken his leg badly and that's what they had to operate on. He's still under anaesthetic but they think he'll be out soon. I don't know much more than that, but they're pleased with how it's gone."

"Oh my god. My poor Sam," I hear her wail. I think I can hear Ron's voice in the background, then Janie comes on the phone. "Is Alice still there?"

I sit up. Nod to Dad. Janie's already been through enough this evening. And I feel a big sister's responsibility towards her. "Hi, Janie."

"What did you say, Alice? What have they done?"

"I don't know many details," I tell her. "All I know is they've operated on his leg and they're pleased with how it's gone. And we should be able to see him soon," I add, brightened by the thought.

"We'll be there soon," she says. "As soon as we can."

I end the call, lean against Dad, and let the tears come.

In time, the nurse returns. "You can see him now. But he is still anaesthetised. You can expect him to come round shortly but he's likely to feel quite woozy and perhaps even quite sick. I'll be in to check on him but if he wakes up please press the buzzer."

She leads the way, Dad and I hot on her heels. We follow her past a window with blinds drawn on the other side and she opens the door, allowing us in to a small, private room where my beloved Sam is lying on a bed, attached to a drip. Some of his beautiful curly hair has been shaved and a medical dressing pressed in its place. He also has two black eyes, and his right leg is already in plaster.

"It was a bad break," she says, "but we've been able to do a scan and ascertain that there are no internal injuries. He was very lucky, from what I hear."

I exhale. I look at Sam. The machine next to him emits regular, reassuring beeps.

"And he's going to be OK?" I ask.

"I think so. He's been through a lot but, as I say, there's no sign of any other major injury. Just the cut on his head, which looks nasty but is really superficial, and some other bumps and bruises." I'm awed at her ability to be so casual about it all. But, of course, she's seen much worse – and this is not her fiancé she's talking about. She smiles again. "I think he's been quite lucky. And he seems a strong young man," she smiles.

"He is. Thank you. Thank you so much."

I pull a chair up to the bed and sit down heavily, resting my head next to Sam's side and allowing the tears to fall again. I hear voices outside the room and look up. Karen.

"Sam's mum's here," the nurse says, putting her head round the door. "But I'm afraid we can only allow two visitors at a time."

"I'll go back to the waiting room," says Dad, putting a hand on my shoulder.

"OK." Really, I want him to stay. I don't want to be in here with Karen, who looks distraught, but of course she wants to be with her son. I see Janie peering over her shoulder and I give her a small smile. Ron, behind her, winks at me kindly. They disappear, with Dad, and the nurse comes in, checking a few readings and Sam's oxygen saturation.

"Looks good," she smiles at me before leaving Karen and me and an unconscious Sam.

I move back so Karen can see her son properly. "Oh Sam," she says. "My poor boy." She kisses his cheek.

Something shifts in me. I see myself, looking in on Ben earlier. Kissing his soft cheek. Things have improved dramatically between Karen and me, and between her and Sam, over the last couple of years, but now I really feel like I know her. I know how she feels.

What's done is done, and we can't change the past. Anyway, all of us parents are just making it up as we go. And we all make mistakes. What I hope is that most people are lucky enough to have parents who love them, and right now I see just how much Karen loves her son.

I put my arm round her shoulder, and I hug her, and we cry into each other's shoulders for some time.

"What are you two sobbing about?" I hear from behind me and I turn rapidly.

"Sam!" I exclaim.

He looks tired, his two black eyes only exacerbating things, but he has a small smile on his lips.

"Sam!" Karen echoes.

"Are you crying about me?" he asks.

"Yes," I say. "You idiot. Of course we are. What the hell were you doing, out on that cliff in the dark and the wind and the rain?"

Karen puts her hand on my arm. "There'll be time for that later," she says gently. And I don't feel annoyed at her interference. I know she's right.

She stands back so that I can go to him.

"Are you alright?" I ask, determined not to cry anymore.

"I think so, I…" he looks about him, then down to his leg. "Oh."

"Yes, oh. It's broken," I explain unnecessarily.

A wave of nausea washes over me but I ignore it. I shouldn't have drunk so much last night but now is not the time for a hangover.

"Oh my god, Sam," I say. "I was scared I'd lost you."

"You haven't lost me. That will never happen," he says.

"Promise?" I ask, although I know he can't promise that, not really.

"Promise," he smiles, and his voice sounds dry and croaky. He stops for a moment, remembering something. "What about Jonathan? Have you found him? Is he OK?"

"He's fine," I say. "I'll tell you all about it when you've had time to come round a bit more." I kiss him softly on his forehead, right next to the dressing.

"Ouch."

"Serves you right for being so stupid," I say, but I'm smiling. "Karen," I turn to her, "come and say hello to your son."

I stand up to let Karen sit on the chair and I open the door to the corridor. I spy a different nurse to the earlier one. "He's awake."

She smiles at me. "I'll be right in."

Karen insists on taking the good news to the three in the waiting room. I sit gratefully next to Sam, holding his hand.

"Can you stop staring at me?" he smiles.

"Was I? Sorry! I just…" I can't get the words out.

"I'm the one who should be sorry," he says. "I didn't mean any of this to happen…" he gestures towards his prone body and his plastered leg.

"Of course you didn't!"

"I've really fucked things up, haven't I?"

"No, you haven't," I rush to reassure him.

"We're meant to be getting married in a few days' time," he reminds me.

"Oh. Yeah." I hadn't forgotten, exactly, but the wedding isn't the first thing on my mind.

"And haven't you got your yoga week starting today?"

Shit.

"Yes, don't worry, I'm sure Julie can cover things there. We'll work it out."

"And Jonathan? Is he really OK? I went after him. I felt bad. I…"

"He's OK. He feels as awful as you do about all this. Don't worry about it now, though. Don't worry about any of it. Just get better, please. Keep your energy for that."

"I'll do my best. I love you, Alice, and I really am sorry."

22

Later on the Sunday, when I am truly satisfied that Sam is OK and not about to take a sudden, unexpected turn for the worse, Dad drives me back home.

It's another quiet journey. We are just too tired to speak.

Dad makes a valiant attempt at first: "Quite a weekend, eh?"

"Yep."

"You going to be OK, love?"

"I think so. I'm just so tired now."

"Mum says you'll be exhausted emotionally as well as physically," he says proudly, glad to have an understanding of the state I'm in.

"I'd say that about covers it, not to mention the after-effects of the hen party last night. I'm just glad I stopped drinking early."

When I'd spoken to Julie, she had not sounded too great. "Do these kids have volume controls?" she'd groaned. I could hear Ben's voice in the background and a cackle of laughter from Zinnia. Once that girl really does start moving, we're going to have to watch out. It is probably a good thing we'll be in our new house one day soon. Together, my son and Julie's daughter could be a terrible force to be reckoned with. At the same time, it seems a bit of a shame. They're kind of like siblings at the moment. But I am certain they'll still see a lot of each other. They are unlikely to have any choice in the matter.

"Check the back of their heads," I laughed.

"You're thinking of Eagle Eye Action Man."

"Easy mistake."

"I'm so glad Sam's OK," Julie said.

"You and me both."

"And Jon."

"Yep, and Jon."

"He will be now, I think. Janie, too. But they need to sort out what they want to do with their lives. And Jonathan needs to go and see a doctor. Or a counsellor. Or something."

"I wonder if he will."

"Well make sure he does!" Knowing Julie, she will.

Thinking of Julie's forthrightness turned my mind to Lydia. I had messaged her late in the night just to say Jonathan was OK. She'd slipped my mind but judging by her fast response she'd been waiting up.

Thank god for that, she'd typed back. **I'm so sorry, Alice, for everything. And now for ruining your hen night as well!**

You don't know the half of it, I'd thought. I didn't mention anything about Sam. It is no business of hers. Besides, I really didn't have the energy to go over it all again, not then.

Don't worry about it, Lydia. Now get some sleep! x

I added a kiss in an attempt to let her know I wasn't angry at her; not really. She's just young and trying to make her way in the world; trying to stamp her mark on it. In a very ill-thought-out way, that's for sure, but as I said, she's young.

"Why don't you try and get some sleep, Alice?" Dad asks now, turning briefly to me.

"It doesn't feel right. You've been up all night, too."

"Well, I had a couple of hours' in the waiting room, actually. Once I knew Sam was OK," he adds quickly.

I lean my head against the window, grateful for the car's air conditioning because, in a sharp contrast to last night's downpour, the day is bright and hot, as if the weather is distancing itself from its terrible behaviour over the last twenty-four hours. *No, no, you must be mistaken. I've been good as gold, me.* Even the ground, which should be sodden and gloopy, is as dry as ever, cracked and dusty. Like it hasn't seen rain in weeks. Conspiring with the weather.

We take the A38 as far as Bodmin then change onto the A30. I can't really sleep, I realise, so watch for the road signs with the names that I love as we head home. Merrymeet, Liskeard, Screech Owl Sanctuary, Indian Queens, St Columb, Zelah, Marazanvose, Wheal Rose, Trevarnon, Lelant Saltings. The familiar wind turbines, adding an almost space-like feel to the landscape. The moors and the rocky spaces where lakes sit like mirrors, as still as the sky.

Is it any wonder that Cornwall's population swells from a few hundred thousand to a few million every summer? Or that there's a popular opinion amongst its native people that it should be devolved: a proud nation in its own right?

I fall into a kind of trance as we head deep into the county I love, which I've come to call home. And maybe I do doze off, for a few minutes here and there. At one point I certainly find that I've dribbled a little and I like to think I wouldn't do that if I was fully conscious. Not yet, at least.

When we get to Julie and Luke's, it is empty and I'm

187

grateful. They're all at Amethi, I know. Julie messaged me to say she'd be welcoming the yoga guests and Luke was taking the kids up there to play in the woods.

Jon's there, too, she had added, **and Janie. They're planning on having a picnic.**

It struck me how easily, how quickly, Jon's mood seemed to have changed. But it's not that easy, I know. He'll be trying his hardest to return to normality and make amends for all the worry he caused last night. I hope he and Janie can work it out but it's up to them now.

I have my own problems to worry about; not least, our wedding next week and the fact that my groom is currently laid up in bed in the Plymouth hospital with his leg in plaster and a bald patch on the side of his head. How the hell is he going to get down that woodland path at the Longhouse? Assuming he's allowed out of hospital by then.

I must phone Sophie, too. I did speak to her this morning; Sam did as well. We put the loudspeaker setting on, the phone resting on Sam's good leg. Just like Ben, she had slept all night with no idea whatsoever of the drama that had been unfolding.

"You're in hospital? In Plymouth?" she'd said, sounding sleepy and confused, then increasingly worried.

"Yes, but I'm OK," said Sam. "Just very tired."

"And very leg-broken," I said.

"You've broken your legs?"

"Just one of them," Sam said, as if that made everything OK. "I'm going to miss lunch with you, I'm so sorry."

"Don't worry, Dad. We'll do it again soon. And I'll see you next week, at the wedding."

I don't think it even occurred to her that having a

wedding might now be difficult. Sam and I had looked at each other and both decided not to say anything.

"I just wish I hadn't missed the chance to spend some time with you, Soph," Sam said.

"Don't worry, Dad," she said again, and it occurred to me that to Sophie there is nothing to worry about. There is all the time in the world. She knows Sam is there for her, always, and she's looking out, not in, or back. She's seeing where she might go next; thinking about her friends, and parties – and possibly her studies. And that's as it should be. She's happy and confident and looking forward to her life. I wouldn't want it any other way, and neither would Sam. No matter how much he misses her.

I shower and put on some clean clothes then I head over to Jim's to collect Meg. She is very excited to see me and I put my arms round her, letting her lick my ear. I'm equally glad to see her.

"How's she been?" I ask.

"Oh, just perfect," he says. "In fact, I'm thinking of getting one of my own. It's crossed my mind a lot lately and I think this weekend has decided me. How's Sam?" he looks suddenly concerned.

"He's OK. Or he's going to be."

"And how are you? You must be shattered."

"I am. But I'm going to head up to Amethi, say hello to everyone, grab Ben and go home. Bathtime and bed at seven. For both of us."

"It's a bit early for me," Jim grins. "And I don't know what Sam would think about us having a bath together."

"In your dreams!" I smile, glad of the excuse to laugh. "I mean for me and Ben."

"Can't blame me for trying," Jim says. "I'm glad the

lad's OK. He's a bit like a second son to me."

"I know."

"And can the wedding still go ahead?"

"I don't know. I hope so, though. We've paid upfront for it. And, of course, I want to marry Sam. I should have said that bit first!"

"It'll work out, Alice. I'm sure it will."

"Thanks, Jim. I'd better get going. I'll see you next week, I hope."

"At the wedding?"

"Exactly. See you next week at the wedding."

Let's give positive thinking a go. See where that gets us.

23

I don't know if I've ever appreciated the drive into Amethi more. It feels like entering another world. As I emerge through the trees, I imagine what it feels like to be a guest arriving here for the first time. It is at its very best today; the leaves and hedgerows so green and brilliant in the sunshine; the air teeming with tiny flying creatures, darting this way and that above the wildflower meadows; butterflies flitting about and chasing each other, dancing against the backdrop of a picture-perfect sky. There are a couple of dragonflies, too, showing off their iridescent colours as they whizz from place to place.

I can see Luke's head, tall above the waving grasses of one of the meadows. He looks up and raises his hand but appears to be preoccupied with something on a much lower level. I assume it is one or other, or both, of our children. I wave back and drive slowly and carefully along the dusty, bumpy track into the car park. When I've pulled up, I open the door and let Meg out. She runs off excitedly, sniffing the air, her nose down and her tail held high. I take a few moments, to breathe it all in, and to let my thoughts and feelings settle. I am exhausted and feel edgy after all that's happened in the last day or so. But I need to put it behind me for the next couple of hours and put my best work face on.

Breathe in. Breathe out. Breathe iiin. Breathe ouuuuuuuut.

"Alice?"

I should have known that my time alone would not be long. It's Jon's voice I've heard and I turn round, a smile

191

placed carefully on my face. "Hello."

"Oh, Alice," his face crumples and I stand up, moving towards him. I put my arms round him and he puts his head on my shoulder.

"I am so, so sorry."

"Shhh," I say. "You said sorry last night and that's enough. You don't need to keep saying it."

"But Sam…"

"… is OK."

"He's in hospital!" he exclaims indignantly.

"Yes, he is, but he won't be forever."

"But it's my fault."

"No, it's not. Not really. I know you must feel like that. But it was Sam's decision to go galumphing up to the coastal path, not yours."

"But he was looking for me."

"Yes, and so were the search and rescue crew, and the lifeboat crew. Sam had already been told to go home because he wasn't going to be any use in the state he was in. And also, he shouldn't have been so nasty to you. How's Janie?" I want to change the subject. I do mean those things I've told Jon, I think, but more than anything, I don't want to get into all this now. I haven't had a chance to really think it all through myself, and find out my real thoughts and feelings on the matter; and besides, I'm at work. I need to be professional. And I'm grateful that I have something else to focus on for the time being. In all honesty, everything feels like a bit of a mess, personally, and I need some proper time to think it all through.

"She's OK," he says. "She's been great."

"Good." I smile. "Now, remember a few weeks back when we talked and you said she wasn't happy? Do you think it was more because you haven't been happy?"

"Possibly," he smiles slightly. "I don't always see things very clearly. And I know I should have told her about Lydia being in contact. But I was worried how she'd react. And if I am very honest, which I have promised Janie I will be, I didn't feel like I had the energy to deal with any fallout from it."

Yet again, I think, a situation which could have been so much better if people had just been honest with each other. We do it all the time; hold things back in an attempt to protect somebody but end up making things worse than they were to begin with.

"I'm glad things are looking a bit better, Jon. And thanks for doing the breakfasts at the Sail Loft this morning."

"It's the least I could do."

Yes, I think, it is. But I know that's just mean.

"Come on," I say, putting my arm through his. "I need to go and do the meet and greet."

"Mummy!" I hear as Jon and I are making our way to the Mowhay; the communal area, where the yoga classes will be held. The bifold doors are open and I can see a lot of the week's guests are there already, sitting at the wooden tables, soaking up the sun. Before I can get to them, Ben's reached me and is grabbing onto my legs.

"Hello, little man!" I say, swinging him up into the air. The absolute purity of his laughter and baby-toothed smile is enough to put a lump in my throat but now is not the time. And everything is OK, I tell myself.

I carry him with me as I go to greet the guests. I know many of them already and they greet me like I'm an old friend. I always think these events that we run; the writing and the yoga, can create strong bonds very quickly. They open people up. I'm glad to see so many smiling faces and I move among them, chatting and catching up, between a hundred interruptions from Ben.

"Right, you," I say, "can you see Meg over there?"

She's lying in the shade of a bush, panting.

"Mm-hmm."

"Can you go and sit with her for a few minutes while I just go and see Lizzie? I've just got a little bit of work to do then we'll go home, I promise."

"Watch *Dinosaur Train*?"

"Yes, watch *Dinosaur Train*."

Somehow, nothing seems more attractive than getting back home and lying on the sofa with Ben while he watches his current favourite programme and I maybe have the chance to close my eyes for a few minutes. Of course, it's unlikely to work out like that. He'll be running trucks up and down my legs, or bouncing on my stomach, but it can't hurt to dream.

I see Christine, who has been here with her family and on a previous yoga course, spot Ben and go to talk to him while he makes his way to Meg. They sit together on the grass next to the dog, who wags her tail lazily and drops back onto her side so they can stroke her belly.

I turn towards the Mowhay, which seems cool and dark in contrast to the bright heat of the afternoon.

"Hi, Alice," Lizzie is inside, checking the speakers and the lighting. Her back is to me, yet somehow she knows I'm here. She is dressed in loose patterned trousers and a vest, and from behind she could easily be mistaken for somebody half her age. Her body is so finely tuned, she's probably fitter than most women half her age. She turns and gives me a hug. "Julie says you've been having a bit of a time."

"You could say that."

"Oh man, sounds like a mess."

"It was," I agree. "It is. But it's as much of a mess as I let

194

it be," I say determinedly.

"That's the way, my girl. Now, they're all here, the full complement, and I wondered if you want to get on with the welcome sooner rather than later, get your little one to bed, then let it all wash over you. I've brought you some tea to help you sleep tonight, too."

"Nothing dodgy, is it?" I grin.

"No, nothing like that, unless…?"

"No thanks, Lizzie. I don't think that would be a good idea. But I do think it's a good idea to do the welcome soon, thank you. And for the tea as well. That's really thoughtful of you."

"Yes, well, it all sounds incredibly stressful, and I know you've got the wedding coming up as well…"

"Maybe…"

"It'll work out, Alice." Her words echo Jim's. "As the universe intended." He didn't mention that bit.

"I hope so."

"Trust me. Trust the universe."

That's all well and good, I think, and I want to trust the universe, but it's not like everything always works out, is it? And many people have a truly awful time of things; where's the universe for them, eh? I have the same problem with all this as I do with religion, really. It doesn't seem to me like life is fair, and if there's some higher being – or more than one higher being – then it seems to be remiss in some cases.

"This looks great," I say, not wanting to get into all that. The room really does look beautiful. There are vases filled with beautiful, bold flowers in golds, oranges and yellows: marigolds, roses, dahlias and daisies. Bunches of last year's lavender, which Lizzie harvested, dried and stored, tied with twine. The windowsills bear planters with lemon balm, mint and rosemary. In the centre of the long wooden table, which has been moved way back, is an arrangement of flowers and candles. "I love the table decoration."

"It's a mandala. A prayer circle. The candles represent the light of the sun and the circle the endlessness of time and the ever-turning year."

"It's lovely."

"Its intention is healing," she says. "It seems to me there are a few round here who need it."

I think of Jon, and of Janie. And Sam, of course, who needs physical healing but perhaps also spiritual and emotional healing, to get through this period of transition in his relationship with Sophie.

"For you as well, Alice," Lizzie says, as if she's seen me run through the list in my mind. "And Julie. You need to heal from the past, though I think you're doing very well in that respect. And Julie is still aching inside, though she has the gift of Zinnia."

Bloody hell. I'm going to be in tears again in a moment.

"Lizzie," I kiss her cheek. "You are lovely. I have to keep my work head on right now, though. Shall we do this?"

"Yes. Let's," she smiles.

There is a subtle scent on the air, from all the different flowers in here, which will become more intense if the doors are closed but is perfect as it is. Delicate fragrances dancing on the gentle currents created by the ever-so-slight breeze and our movement as we walk across the room.

I follow her to the open doors, where she jingles some bells that she's pulled from who knows where. The people gathered turn towards us. Julie is here as well, with Zinnia in her arms. I can see Ben, Christine and Meg are just where they were a few minutes ago and I send a smile their way before I begin to speak.

"Welcome, everyone," I say, feeling their faces turned towards me, as the sunlight pours over us all. The air is still and a fly buzzes past my ear. "Thank you so much for coming to what promises to be another special time for us all. It is lovely to see so many familiar faces, and some new ones, too." I look to Julie, who smiles. "Over there, we have Julie, who many of you will already know. She's my business partner at Amethi and an amazing chef. As you can see, she has her hands full, literally, with her gorgeous daughter at the moment, so the cooking is shared with another talented chef, Jonathan, who is busy in the kitchen right now, preparing this evening's feast. I'm very sorry I won't be able to join you tonight but I will be around throughout the week and I will certainly be here to celebrate the solstice with you all."

For weeks, I've been planning what I'd say to welcome everyone to this retreat, and how I'd throw in that it's my wedding day on Friday. In my daydreams, I'd imagined basking in the congratulations and good wishes. Now, I just don't want to mention it. I don't want to risk telling everyone only for it not to go ahead.

"Thank you, Alice," Lizzie says, smiling. "Now, I've got a gentle yoga session lined up before tea tonight. And at the risk of sounding like a killjoy, I'd suggest you perhaps step inside and out of the sunlight for a while; into our beautiful Mowhay, where there's iced mint water for those who want it. You can socialise and get to know your fellow yogis a little better, or you might want to go back to your rooms, to ground yourselves and prepare for the week ahead. As Alice said, it's going to be a special one. I'd like you all to get everything you can from it. And I do not want any one of you suffering from heatstroke! Believe me, the Cornish sun can be very hot."

"I know you lot don't consider yourselves English like the rest of us, but I didn't know you'd got your own sun as well!" calls Mike, who has been here for one of the autumn equinox retreats, and enjoys trying to wind Lizzie up.

"There's a lot you don't know, Mike," she grins at him and he takes it in good humour.

Lizzie rings her bells again and, obediently, the gathered people stand up, some slowly stretching. A handful come inside the Mowhay but most disappear off around the corner to their accommodation. I hear their voices drifting back through the hot, heavy air.

"Right," I say. "Thank you, Lizzie. I think I'll take the chance to head home now, if you don't mind? I am sorry to miss this evening."

"Don't give it another thought," she says.

"Julie," I say to my friend, who's replaced Christine on the grass next to Ben. Zinnia is on her knees, her hands in Meg's fur. Meg just lies, patiently, used to being manhandled by these small people and apparently not minding at all. "I think I'm going to make a move."

"I don't blame you. Make sure you get some rest. I'll stay up here but Luke'll be home soon, with Zinnia. He'll mind Ben for you."

"No, that's fine, thanks. To be honest, I can't think of anything I'd like more than hanging out with this little one." I ruffle Ben's hair, which has gone white-blond this summer.

"I get that," says Julie. "Well, I've got everything covered here, and Jon's doing great stuff in the kitchen. I think he's working twice as hard to prove his worth and make amends."

"He doesn't need to do that," I feel bad I didn't really talk to him properly in the car park.

"No, but we might as well take advantage of his guilt!" She grins wickedly and I laugh.

"Come on then, you two," I say to my boy and dog. "Sorry, Zinnia, I'm stealing Meg away from you. We'll see you at home soon."

"Home soon," she agrees.

Julie pulls her onto her knee. "You are too cute!" I think what Lizzie said about Julie still aching inside. I don't imagine that it's easy to get over not being able to have a baby, but I don't doubt the strength of her love for her daughter; not for one minute.

Ben holds my hand as we walk across the gravel to the car, Meg trotting ahead. I wish I'd left the car windows open as it is baking hot inside, so we open the doors for a while and lean against the wall. A small group of gulls fly slowly overhead and I watch their progress until they've passed above the line of trees and are no longer anywhere to be seen. I can hear a gang of sparrows in the hedgerow as well, chattering merrily together.

I feel overcome with tiredness all of a sudden and I am glad when the car has cooled enough that I can strap Ben into his seat then open the boot for Meg to jump in. Then we are off, bumping down the drive and back between the trees. I stop to check for cars then turn onto the road, leaving the alternative reality of Amethi behind me; heading in the direction of the sea, and towards whatever awaits me in the week ahead.

24

It's late afternoon on the solstice and the preceding days have been hot and long. Sam came back from Plymouth on Tuesday, by ambulance. I had wanted to collect him but, as he rightly pointed out, it would be a bit of a squeeze trying to get into the little red car.

"I'd have to have my leg out of the window," he'd smiled. He is sore and bruised from his fall, and his ego is a little bit bruised as well, I'd say. "I know better than to go traipsing off up the cliffs with a bellyful of booze… in the dark, and the rain," he has groaned, more than once.

"Yes, but unfortunately that bellyful of booze was probably telling you something else. And you were worried about Jonathan." *You silly bugger*, I want to add, but I don't. He feels bad enough already.

"The wedding's still going ahead though," he said. "I may have two black eyes, and a broken leg, and… oww… don't worry, I'm fine." That was just him trying to sit up in bed.

Meanwhile, things are progressing with the house sale. We could be moving in as soon as August but Sam's leg is meant to be in plaster for eight weeks. This could make moving tricky – but we've had offers of help from Julie and Luke, David and Martin, and Mum and Dad. We'll manage somehow. And I am so keen to move now; to find our own space. We are all so close, here, and it's lovely, but we do need some space, Sam and I, and Ben and Sophie. I will miss being able to see the sea but I know I'll be able to hear it, and smell it, from our new house.

On Monday night, Shona took me out for a drink or two.

"Sláinte, Alice." She'd ordered a bottle of prosecco and we were sitting out on a balcony at the Olive Branch, overlooking the harbour.

"Thank you, Shona. This is just what the doctor ordered."

"Yeah, it sounds like you've been through the mill. I wanted to do this, as I couldn't make it to your hen do. And I totally understand we can't come to your wedding. You can't invite everyone."

"No, I know. I'd like to, but…"

"No, you wouldn't!" she smiled. "At least, I wouldn't… and I won't. Paul's had that big wedding thing and I'm just not too bothered. I want to marry him, and be married to him. I do want to celebrate it but not with eighty people just for the sake of it. No, you and Sam are doing the right thing. Small and intimate, with just your closest family and friends."

"Thank you, Shona," I said again. I've found it a bit awkward, when people have asked about the wedding and I've wondered if they've been expecting invitations. "And it's true. I think you decide to go for it, with all your aunts and uncles and cousins, and their partners and kids, and your parents' friends, and all that… or else you whittle it down to the bare minimum."

"The bare minimum. I like that idea." Shona's eyes flicked over the harbour, the evening light softening the view, then back to me. "I used to feel threatened by you, you know," she looked at me candidly.

"You…?" This took me by surprise.

"Yes, and not because of anything you'd done. I knew Paul had a real soft spot for you, though. He still does. And he told me what he'd done to help you get Amethi. He really liked you, you know."

"Did he?"

"Yes, and I'm not trying to make you feel awkward, I promise. We all come with baggage, I know that. I just... he used to say your name and I used to hate 'Alice', whoever she was, but then I met you, and Julie, and I couldn't really hate you anymore."

My cheeks were blushing red.

"Sorry!" she smiled. "The drink's gone to my head. I shouldn't have said that."

"No, it's fine. Paul and I, well, it was something and nothing. I met him when I was feeling really quite down about things. Actually, that's not true. I was determinedly not feeling quite down about things but it was this weird year, when everyone seemed to be getting married, and Sam and I had split up for the second time and..."

"And now you're getting married," she interrupted, smiling.

"And so are you and Paul. You are a much better match than he and I ever were, or ever could be. But I think very highly of him, and of you."

"It's strange, this town, isn't it?" Shona's eyes were on the harbour again. The moored boats were barely moving; the night was so still but the water was still moving, gently, lulling the boats to sleep. "I didn't know if I liked it when I first came here. I was glad Paul lived a bit further away. It actually reminds me of home, you know."

"Really?" I'd never thought about where Shona came from.

"Oh aye, I'm from a small Scottish fishing town," she put on a broad accent. "Everybody knows one another and everybody knows everybody else's business."

"It can be like that here, but it's also kind of nice. I come from somewhere a bit bigger; a bit more anonymous. I like the way people look out for each other here."

"I get that. And I've kind of settled back into it, although I'm still glad our house is remote."

"Plus, that is one amazing house."

"It is, isn't it?" she smiled. "I don't think I've ever been so happy. And I love the community here now, you know. Business and otherwise. I love working with you and Julie, and with your parents. There is no way I'd have taken on that work for the Bay."

"Even though I bet Felicity could pay about twice as much as we do?"

"It's not all about that, Alice, and I know you know that."

We sat quietly for a while and I thought about the Bay Hotel, and Lydia. I will have to see her again soon but for now I think it's best we keep our distance.

Paul came to take Shona and me home, pulling up on the harbourside in his shiny convertible.

"Flash bastard," Shona muttered to me and I laughed.

"What are you two giggling about?" Paul asked, as we clambered in.

"Oh, nothing."

"Well, I'm glad you've had a good time." My eyes met his in the mirror and we both smiled. Was he 'the one that got away'? No, I really don't think so. We enjoyed each other's company, and I did fancy him like mad, but that's not enough, is it? And I never loved him. Not like I love Sam. Like I've always loved Sam.

"So is Sam OK?" Paul asked as we headed slowly along the harbour road, turning left into the narrow meandering streets. "Will you still be able to get married this week?"

"I hope so," I said. "I really do."

"If we can help in any way, just let me know." He turned then and smiled at Shona, putting his hand on her knee.

"Thank you," I said, and I sat back and enjoyed the ride through town, people sitting outside the tapas bar looking at us as we passed by. Probably thinking, *Flash bastard!*

When we drew up at Julie and Luke's house, Paul got out and so did Shona. She hugged me. "Have a great wedding day, Alice."

"Thank you, Shona. And thanks for a lovely evening."

"No problem. We'll do it again soon."

"Good luck for Saturday, Alice." Paul's eyes crinkled at me, and he put his hands on my shoulders while Shona got back into the car. "Have a wonderful day. You deserve it."

"Thank you, Paul." I hugged him and thought how lucky I am to have these people in my life. Maybe it's the recent drama, or my upcoming wedding, or the fact that it's solstice week; whatever it is, since Monday night I feel like my emotions have intensified. The slightest thing can have tears flooding to my eyes, but it's a good feeling. I'm very aware of all the wonderful people I have in my life to feel thankful for.

Now, it's the closing section of the last yoga session of the retreat. Lizzie has brought us all outside, with our mats, and we are lying on our backs under the sun, listening to her soothing voice. "On this solstice; the time of the year when there is the most light available to us, this is when we are most present in ourselves, and who we know ourselves to be. The sun represents the light of all life, of all consciousness. Just as the flowers unfurl in its warmth, our souls open to receive its light."

I catch myself just before I doze off, blinking my eyes slightly, even though Lizzie has said to keep them closed. To my left is Janie, and to her left is Jonathan. They surprised us all on Monday morning by asking if they could take part. They have not missed a session since. Jonathan has somehow managed to fit all his work around the yoga sessions, creating beautiful, summery salads with fresh fruit and vegetables grown locally; bountiful loaves of seeded bread; summer puddings and mouth-watering sorbets.

The secret, as it turned out, is Janie, as I discovered when I popped into the kitchen on Tuesday morning. There she was, busily washing a sinkful of tomatoes.

"Oh, hi, Alice."

"Hello," I'd smiled. "What's all this?"

"I've taken the week off. So that Jon and I can spend some time together. And I'm helping him in here so he's got time for the yoga," she had smiled shyly. "I hope that's OK."

"Of course. That's more than OK. I think it's great."

"Yeah, well, we've been talking... a lot. And I think if we're going to make this work we need to make some changes."

"So he's got you helping him in the kitchen?" I teased.

"No, he's... I want to do it. I've done a bit of this before, in Spain, you know. When I was a student. And I know how to make Salmorejo, which is what these are for." She gestured at the tomatoes.

"Salmo...?"

"It's a cold tomato soup. A Spanish speciality. People have it with ham, or boiled egg. I know," she said, spying my expression. "It sounds disgusting! But it works, somehow."

"I'll take your word for it."

"It seemed a perfect choice for today. It's so hot."

Jonathan came whistling through the door. "Hi, Alice." But he had eyes only for Janie, sending one of his brilliant smiles her way.

"Hi, Jon."

Honestly, it's like the last few days and weeks haven't happened. But the difference is, we all know that they have. We know how Jon has been, and that it can't be solved just like that, but it seems to me that between him and Janie they can get through anything.

I turn my head slightly now to take a sneaky look at my nearly-sister-in-law. She has her eyes shut tight against the sun and her breathing is slow and calm. If I'm not much mistaken, she even has a bit of a sun tan, which is a first in as long as I've known her. I turn my face back towards the sky and keep my eyes closed like a good girl. I breathe in and then I sigh. I can't help it. Life feels good.

When the session is over and we have all stood slowly and slightly dazedly, blinking our eyes in the bright sunshine and letting reality return, Lizzie brings us each a glass of cold, iced water decorated with mint leaves. There is a slight taste of cucumber to the water as well. It is incredibly refreshing.

"I'll be lighting the fire soon," says Lizzie. "You are free to do as you please for another hour or so. Except you, Jon," she smiles at our chef. "I believe you have a solstice feast for us all."

"I do," he says. "I'll get back to it." He snaps his heels and salutes smartly, and heads towards the kitchen. Janie catches up with him and takes his hand.

Julie, who has just arrived, sees this and smiles at me. She's been quite emotional herself this week; it's like the weekend's events have brought everyone's priorities into focus. She and Luke have been talking more and more about him leaving his London life behind altogether and I think he will do this in the next couple of months. Which makes me feel less guilty about moving out.

I help Lizzie arrange the wood for the bonfire. "You OK, Alice?"

"I'm fine, thank you."

"You sure? You seem a little bit distracted. I noticed you weren't quite letting yourself go in the meditation."

Damn. She noticed. I should have known she would.

"Yeah, I, well I nearly fell asleep actually, and didn't want to start snoring. I think I was a bit too relaxed."

"It can be hard to get that balance. I guess you've got a lot on your mind."

"I guess I have."

"Your wedding…?"

"Yes," I say, busily stacking a lot of kindling in the heart of the pile. "There is that."

"You're not looking forward to it?"

"I am," I say defensively.

"But it's not how you'd hoped it might be?"

"No. Not really. I mean, I want to marry Sam, of course. Whatever the circumstances. And we've waited so long to be able to do this. But now his leg's in plaster, and he can't really get about. He says he'll crawl if he has to! But I don't want him to have to. And everything hurts him, Lizzie." It's all coming out now. "He should be resting in bed; recovering."

"Can you delay it?"

"No, we can't; not at this late stage. Besides, we've paid for it all upfront."

Lizzie smiles. Closes her eyes. "It'll work out, Alice," she says, just like she did the other day.

"It'll have to," I sigh, and get back to the fire-building.

Most of the guests had gone off to shower and get changed but before long they come drifting back in twos and threes.

Janie appears, as if by instinct, bearing trays of cold drinks. "These are alcoholic," she nods towards some long, cold glasses on one side of the tray, filled with ice, strawberries, and an orange drink. "They're bourbon, ginger beer, lemon juice and rhubarb. The non-alcoholic ones are on the other side, and they're ginger, lime, and lemonade."

I opt for a non-alcoholic one when she reaches me and Lizzie. "Thank you, Janie. You're a bit of a natural at this, you know."

"What? Handing out drinks?"

"No! Just being nice and friendly and welcoming to people." I'd always thought she was very shy and preferred to be in the shadows but actually, given the chance to be a bit more outgoing, she seems to be enjoying it.

"I suppose I get a bit wrapped up in work sometimes, and that can make me a bit inward-looking," she admits. "It's something I'm going to work on," she adds earnestly.

"Janie, you don't have to change a thing," says Lizzie. "You're a beautiful soul."

"Well, I don't know about that," Janie says, scuttling off with her tray.

"She does need to learn how to take a compliment, though," Lizzie smiles. She puts her drink down and lights the fire, then jingles her little handheld bells. "Everyone, the solstice fire is now alight. I know it's still broad daylight, and incredibly hot–" this gets a smattering of laughter, "– but the fire is an important part of the celebration. In countries like Estonia and Latvia, it's believed that the fire scares mischievous spirits who want to ruin the harvest. They also enjoy a bit of fire-jumping, as they do in Spain and Russia as well. Maybe some of you will fancy a go later…?"

More laughter.

I step up now. "While we get the fire going, I believe that Jonathan has been busying laying out the feast we mentioned earlier, so please go on into the Mowhay and help yourselves. You can sit indoors, or out here, and there should be plenty more of these delicious drinks to keep you going too! Cheers, everybody."

There are responding calls of 'Cheers' and they don't have to be told twice to go and eat. It's hungry work, is yoga.

Julie comes across to me and Lizzie. "Shame Sam can't make it," she says.

"I know. He loves these things, but at least he can look after Ben, and he's got Luke and Zinnia for company as well. Besides, he needs to conserve his energy for the wedding."

"I still can't believe you're going ahead, with him in that state!"

"We don't have a lot of choice. It's all paid for and if we don't do it now, we never will. We need all the rest of our cash for our deposit and soon we'll have a mortgage and, you know, I think we'd kind of like a brother or sister for Ben one day…"

"I know. I get it, really. It will be a beautiful day, whatever."

"Even if the groom's got two black eyes?"

"Even then."

When all the guests have emerged with plates piled high, Julie and I go into the Mowhay, promising to bring a plate back for Lizzie. She is very protective of her solstice fires and likes to stay with them at all times, even overnight, including in winter.

There is still plenty to eat and we take thick slices of granary bread; salted tomatoes and thin sticks of cucumbers that were grown in the Amethi vegetable patch. There are delicate tarts filled with crumbly goat's cheese and fig chutney; mixed bean salad and a sticky, spicy rice mixed with raisins and peppers.

For dessert there is cheesecake and fresh fruit salad, as well as an extensive cheeseboard and racks of crackers as well as rolls of golden butter and jars of pickles and chutneys which Jonathan and Julie made in the autumn over the course of a week. We load our plates, and Lizzie's, and go to sit with her near the fire.

It feels so good to be here, on this beautiful day, surrounded by smiling people. I sit quietly while Lizzie and Julie chat, and just soak it all in. The happiness. Laughter and good-humoured conversation. Crickets chirping from the depths of the long, dry grasses. The buzz of insects and the birdsong from the woods. Meg appears, panting, and flops down next to me. I put down my drink and put my arm around her. She sinks against my side.

"You can feel it, can't you?" Lizzie turns to me. "The hum, of the earth."

I smile, and nod. I don't know if she means me, in particular, or more generally. I place my hand on the dry ground to see if I can feel it. Lizzie smiles at me and turns back to Julie. I feed Meg a bit of cheese.

As the evening eventually draws in and the fire begins to come into its own, providing light as well as heat, Lizzie gathers us all together, instructing us to sit in a circle around the fire.

"Thank you, friends, for joining me," she sends a slow deliberate look around the whole circle, making sure to make eye contact with each of us, "on this beautiful evening we celebrate the summer solstice. The longest day of the year. For many, this is a time to celebrate the start of summer. Traditionally, people have focused on the light, life, and a good harvest to come. Tonight, we celebrate all these things, as well as friendship, and love, and our natural surroundings. We are blessed to be held in this beautiful place, Amethi, in this sacred county of Cornwall. I ask you all to join hands in a circle, and close your eyes. Be still, be quiet, for a few moments, and feel the breath of the spirits upon you."

We do as we are asked, and join hands. I have Julie on my left and Jonathan on my right. I send a small smile to both then I close my eyes and concentrate. I can hear the crackle of the fire. A blackbird calling goodnight. My own breath. I feel the warm air around me and the heat radiating from the flames. Then the slightest breeze tiptoes across my face, making the hairs on my arms stand on end. I keep my eyes closed. The breath of the spirits. Lizzie's words. Is this what I can feel, or is it simply the natural movement of the air?

Nobody speaks, for some time. Then there is a familiar sound; a round, clean hum, getting louder and more vibrant, and then Lizzie speaks once more. "Open your eyes, see the world around you. Feel the love of all those present. Give thanks for the sun, for the light of the sun; for the life that comes from the sun."

We remain linked by our hands; all except Lizzie, who walks around the inner circle, skirting the fire, scattering herbs as she goes.

"This is the longest day, the shortest night. This time is Litha, Alban Hefin. Midsummer. The sun god is at his height. Yet darkness hovers as the Wheel rolls ever on. We bid farewell for now to the Oak King, who has so gallantly guided the growing light. As the days grow more abundant, so the nights will draw in more quickly."

I watch her intently as she walks, and talks. There are no pauses, no doubt, in her words. And the soft smell of the fresh herbs, mixed with the white woodsmoke from the fire, adds a dreamlike quality to the proceedings. I look around the circle. Most people have their eyes closed. I notice Jon's are squeezed tightly shut but Janie, like me, is looking around. We catch each other's eye and smile.

"Now, it is time to stand together and face the spirits of the east, the south, the west and the north, and ask them to join us. Turn, my friends, to the east." We do as we are told. In silence and respect. I remember the first time we did this, at a winter solstice, back before Ben was born. Julie, I seem to recall, found it amusing at first, and we had both been unsure what to expect, but what we had definitely not expected was how moved we both were. Lizzie speaks, her voice strong and true. "Now bow your heads, and show your respect to the spirits. And we turn to the south, and do the same. Acknowledge their presence in the universe, and their gifts in our lives. To the west... and finally to the north."

The breeze picks up, as I have known it do before, and some of the herbs Lizzie scattered are lifted and carried towards our feet and towards the flames.

"Now we call in the Goddess, who at this most fertile time of year bears the sun god's child. Everything is at its fullest."

She looks at me and I smile but although Lizzie smiles back, I feel like she is not quite with us; just for a moment. Then she walks back around the circle, not breaking eye contact with me. If it wasn't Lizzie, I'd feel unnerved, but then she looks away, and begins to talk again.

"Some say the veil between this world and the fae is thin right now... that the fae come out to play their tricks, enlivened by the energy of life itself. It is no coincidence that Shakespeare filled his *Midsummer Night's Dream* with faeries and mischief. I'd like to read to you, a little of Oberon's speech, when he plans to wreak havoc on his own queen, Titania:

"I know a bank where the wild thyme blows,
Where oxlips and the nodding violet grows,
Quite over-canopied with luscious woodbine,
With sweet musk-roses and with eglantine:
There sleeps Titania sometime of the night,
Lull'd in these flowers with dances and delight.

"But all's well that ends well, for the humans and the faeries. And I'd like to invite Jonathan to read the closing speech, spoken by perhaps the most mischievous, but well-meaning, Robin Puck."

I glance at Jon, who looks slightly surprised, but nods his agreement and steps forward. Janie and I step closer to each other, join hands and reconnect the circle.

Lizzie smiles at Jonathan, puts her hand on his shoulder and gives him a piece of paper. He clears his throat, looks around nervously, but his eyes settle on Janie's. He smiles, then looks at the paper and begins to read aloud.

"If we shadows have offended,
Think but this, and all is mended:
That you have but slumbered here
While these visions did appear.
And this weak and idle theme,
No more yielding but a dream,
Gentles, do not reprehend.
Give me your hands if we be friends.
And Robin shall restore amends."

Lizzie has cut short this speech but I think I can see her motivation and so can Jon. In fact, I think he is close to tears. Janie drops my hand and goes to hug him. She whispers something in his ear and leads him back to the circle.

Lizzie smiles beneficently. "Thank you, Jonathan. That was beautiful. And now, I have mead and honey cake to share with you all. Some intense sweetness for this summer evening. You can unlink the circle and feel free to sit. Thank you."

The attention is swiftly taken away from Jonathan as Lizzie hands out slices of a deliciously golden, sticky honey cake and small cups of an amber-coloured drink. We all sit quietly, contemplatively; the odd murmured conversation going on. I gaze into the flames and Julie moves ever so slightly closer to me. I lean against her and she rests her head on mine.

When the last crumb has been eaten and sticky fingers wiped ineffectively on the grass, Lizzie speaks again. "And now, while we remain in our circle, I would like you all to stay in your places for just a little while longer, and share with us all something for which you are grateful. Big or small. Anything you feel comfortable saying in a group. Alice, would you start?"

"OK," I say, needing only a moment to think. "I am grateful for this opportunity, to spend evenings like this with people like you."

There are smiles around the group at this and I feel like it was a cheesy thing to say but it was true. Julie says she is grateful for family and friends. Janie shyly says the same, and looks at Jonathan.

"Life," he says. "I'm grateful for life. And for love."

He seems so utterly different to the panic-stricken, pained man of the weekend. How is it possible that was just a handful of days ago? I want to hug him but will wait until later. Instead, I concentrate on being in the moment and, at the risk of sounding like a total hippy, the feeling of love which has washed right through me.

In time, Lizzie asks us to stand and we turn back through the circle, to the spirits in reverse. Thanking them, and asking them to be with us when we need them.

Then we are free to relax, and to mingle once more, while the flames dance between us and blow tiny kisses of ash into the sky.

As the sun slowly, slowly disappears behind the line of trees, I breathe deeply and slowly. I don't want this moment, or this feeling, to end. But I will try to carry it with me as the world keeps on turning and life moves on, as it must; as it always does.

25

The Longhouse looks absolutely beautiful. It is decked with tiny twinkling lights, as are the trees and the woodland clearing, where the chairs are wrapped in a cream silk-like fabric and there is an archway decorated with cream, orange and yellow roses. George has outdone himself – "With a lot of help from Imogen," he said. Christian says George is the most loved-up person he knows ("Even in comparison with you and Sam.")

I haven't felt that we have been so loved up lately. Not since Ben was born, which I suppose is natural, and definitely not since Sophie went away. It's been a hard time and I don't suppose it's possible to be all 'hearts and flowers' when life is getting you down, as it has been for Sam. However, I think that last weekend was a bit of a wake-up call for us both.

Yesterday morning, I fell apart a little. It was at the beach, at the final gathering of the yoga retreat, which Lizzie had tagged onto the end of the course.

It wasn't part of the plan, this early morning meeting, and I had wanted to stay in bed, to catch up on some sleep and begin to prepare for Ben's little birthday party in the afternoon, not to mention my wedding the following day.

However, I'd been so moved by the solstice ceremony that I didn't want to miss out on this final celebration. And Lizzie had given it the hard sell: "Solstice is the time to praise the sun. To stand on the shore where earth, sea and sky meet. A time of in-between, of joining times, thankful for what we have and what is to come. What could be better the day before your wedding, Alice? Particularly given what you've been through this week."

And so I'd set my alarm, super alert the moment it clicked on so that I could switch it off and leave Sam sleeping. He is not resting very well anyway, although I think he has become a bit more used to his leg being pretty much immobile. He normally sleeps on his front, though, and he can't very well do that at the moment. In the soft morning light, which was already beginning to soak through the curtains and saturate the room, I looked at my husband-to-be. His forehead ever-so-slightly less than smooth and his poor bruised skin around his eyes, now yellowing slightly at the edges.

I dressed as quietly as possible, pulling on cropped jeans, a t-shirt and a hoodie, and tiptoed to the front door with my sandals in my hand. Dreading waking either Ben or Zinnia, which would put a dampener on the proceedings. Meg looked up, surprised but pleased to see me about so early, her tail thumping on the floor.

"Come on, girl," I whispered.

Please don't bark, please don't bark.

Julie had opted out of the morning celebration so it was just me and Meg leaving the house, greeted by the incomparable sight of the town in all its early morning summer glory. With the sky already infused with the colours of day, it would not be long until the sun made its appearance. I walked quickly downhill, Meg off her lead in the quiet streets but staying close by my side. I tried to keep an eye on the sea and the sky as I went; drinking in the view.

For once, there were barely any surfers to be seen, and just a handful of people – *all Amethi people*, I thought proudly – gathered some way down towards the shore, where the sand was still wet from the now retreating sea. Meg scampered a little way off, sniffing the air and the sand excitedly, as if she'd never been to the beach before.

"Alice!" Lizzie said warmly and hugged me. Many of the others followed suit.

"I feel so lucky that I get to do this for work!" I said. "And that I get to meet so many lovely people. I hope you'll all think about coming back next year?"

"I'm all ready to book again!" said Christine.

"I'm so glad. Ben will be delighted, too," I squeezed her arm.

"Now," Lizzie spoke loud and clear, "in just a few moments, the sun will begin to make an appearance above the horizon, sharing its light with the earth and the sea. And at this crucial time at the centre of the year, and the seasons, the Holly King is waiting, ready to step forward and take the crown from the Oak King. At this turning of the year, we know that even as the sun rises, we are already turning towards darker days. But this is also a time of abundance. The height of summer is still to come. Please, let's take each other's hands again, and form a circle, be quiet for a while, thankful for the months which have passed, and feel the blessings of the day and the months ahead."

We did as we were bid, and I stood between Lizzie and Christine. My back was to the sea but I was sure I could feel a gradual warmth on the back of my neck.

Lizzie, though she was also facing away from the horizon, after a minute or two said, "She is risen."

We released each other's hands and I turned to see that Lizzie was right. The full shape of the sun; all orange and burnished gold, was now visible above the horizon. On the quiet beach, sea birds pitter-pattered along the shoreline, leaving delicate footprints in the sand. Meg trotted around nearby but her presence didn't seem to bother them. A group of cormorants took it in turns to stretch their wings on the rocks that jut out into the water. The ever-present gulls were rising into the air, high above the town, their wings glowing in the morning light.

"You knew the sun had risen," I said admiringly to Lizzie.

"I could feel it. Couldn't you?"

"Yes, I think I could."

"I knew you would."

Lizzie poured herbal tea from three large flasks she'd brought with her and we laid blankets on the sand, sitting to sip our drinks, most of us quietly contemplative, lost in our own thoughts.

It was then that everything seemed to hit me. Without warning, I found myself in floods of tears. Quiet, silent tears, that nobody would notice, I hoped. My mind leapt back to Saturday night and early Sunday morning and finally I was hit fully by the reality that I had come so close to losing Sam.

My stomach twisted into a deep knot of fear, even though I knew Sam was safe at home, hopefully harnessing the healing powers of sleep. But I had a sudden vision of what had happened to him; searching earnestly for Jonathan; kicking himself for having been so hasty and aggressive towards him. The night had been so dark and the rocks and path must have been so slippery. As the flashlight function was still on when Julie and Luke found his phone, he must have been trying to pick his way along the path. He can't remember exactly what happened but Luke went back along the path the next day and said there is a huge slide mark in the mud, where the path comes close to the cliff edge, and presumably Sam lost his footing and fell down there. He was lucky the tide was out, as those rocks can become fully covered by the sea. If they had been, he'd be gone.

All of that hit me as I sat and looked at the sun. I should have been feeling happy, I thought; excited about the wedding, but right then I couldn't even think about that. All I could think was, *what if?* What if Sam had died? My heart would be broken. Ben and Sophie would have lost their dad. And for all of Sophie's newfound independence, I know full well that if Sam died she would fall to pieces. What would it mean to Ben? I thought of that little boy, who I hoped would also still be fast asleep, not yet old enough to wake super-early with birthday excitement.

I must have let out some kind of sob, or Lizzie used her super senses to notice I was upset. She reached out, put her hand on my arm, her eyes meeting mine.

I nodded. Gulped. *I'm at work,* I told myself. Though it didn't feel like work. But all the people around me apart from Lizzie were paying guests. And the thought of them seeing me upset stopped me in my tracks. Stopped the tears, at the very least. I will deal with this later, I told myself. Though how I was going to fit it in around Ben's birthday celebration and the final preparations for the wedding, I had no idea. Whose idea was it to have so much going on in this one week? Oh yes. Mine.

As the sun rose higher, it seemed to pull us with it. Gradually, we all stood, brushing sand off our clothes. Handshakes and hugs as people said goodbye, and thanked Lizzie and me for such a wonderful week. Some were going straight home, having packed their bags ready for an early start. Some were heading back to Amethi to clear up and enjoy their last chance for a breakfast cooked by Jonathan.

I walked with Lizzie slowly across the sand.

"You OK now?" she asked.

"Yeah, sort of. I guess it all caught up with me."

"That's to be expected. You haven't had a chance to stop this week."

"No, and now I need to get home to the birthday boy."

"He's growing up! Time for another, soon."

"Ha! One thing at a time, eh? Thanks for another amazing week, Lizzie. Now go and get some rest, eh?"

"I will. Back on the beach, I think. Once I've waved this lot off."

We stood and waved as the cars started up one by one and I felt a little sadness, as I always do at the end of a retreat. They're such a magical time. But there's always another to look forward to.

I steeled myself for the steep walk home and picked up some croissants and pains au chocolat from the little bakers on the corner, which was just opening for the day. Meg stayed outside while I walked into the warm shop, the smell of baking making my stomach rumble.

"First one in, Alice!" said Michael.

"Brilliant. The thought of these will keep me going on my way home."

Soon, Sam and I would have our own place to call home. No longer relying on other people (unless you count the bank lending us a couple of hundred thousand, as Sam likes to point out).

I walked briskly, Meg matching my pace effortlessly, unwilling to stop for fear of not being able to get going again, but also increasingly filled with a desire to get to my boy; to be there when he woke on his second birthday. Enjoy the abundance of warm pyjamaed cuddles he happily dishes out. As I opened the door cautiously, Meg nosed her way in before me, heading straight for her drinking bowl in the kitchen. Other than that, all was quiet and still.

I followed Meg through, putting the paper bags from the bakery on the counter.

In the dining room, a pile of presents for Ben lay on the table. I rearranged them, smiling fondly, imagining his excitement at the sight. And then I heard him. "Mummy?" A shuffling sound. A little pair of feet on the landing floor.

"Hello birthday boy!" I was up the stairs as fast as could be, swinging him up into my arms. "You're two today!"

"I'm two!" he agreed happily.

"Who's two?" I heard Sam's sleepy voice from our room.

"Me!" Ben shouted, wriggling down from my arms and into the bedroom.

"Never! Ow!" Sam laughed as Ben scrambled onto the bed, using his plaster cast for support.

"Are you OK?" I asked, kissing him.

"Yeah, never been better," he grinned.

I decided to move the presents and the breakfast into our bedroom, where Luke, Julie, Zinnia and Meg soon joined us, getting crumbs everywhere but filling the room with laughter. I couldn't help thinking, if it was a challenge for Sam to get downstairs to see Ben open his presents, how on earth was he going to be able to get up the next day and get to the Longhouse to get married? But the walk home after the beach had given me time to think. I had a plan.

***

Now, Sam and I look at each other. I want to kiss him but this is the most important part of the day. The vows.

The celebrant speaks slowly and deliberately and I repeat the words after her. Sam does the same. Finally, he leans forward and kisses me. Our mouths join for perhaps a little longer than those watching might consider polite then we draw apart and smile.

On the screen, Shona and Paul are still kissing, to the apparent delight of those gathered around. As opposed to those watching with us. For we decided to delay our wedding. Sam took some persuading, but to me it didn't feel right to go ahead. Had we done so, he would have been in pain, or at the very least uncomfortable, and not able to enjoy the day. Luckily, I knew the perfect couple, who might leap at the chance to take our place.

"Really?" Shona had asked. Then "Really?" again – this time higher-pitched and with fast-growing excitement.

"Yes, really," I said. "But only if you and Paul think it's the right thing for you both. There is no pressure, I promise. I know there's no time, to get people together. But I also know you wanted it small and intimate."

And small and intimate it is, with Paul's children, his mum and his ex-wife, and Shona's sister and brother and their families, who pulled out all the stops to get to Cornwall in time.

"Small and intimate except it's being live-streamed around the world," Sam had said slightly sarcastically.

"Well, you know, she is in PR…"

And it's a beautiful day for them. I can't deny feeling a little bit gutted that it's not our beautiful day, but it wouldn't have been the same for us. I don't know what we'd have done if Paul and Shona hadn't gone for it. We'd have lost our money, I suppose. I had made up my mind, that we should not go ahead. No matter what Sam said. The idea of a broken-legged, bruised and sore-ribbed bridegroom might seem romantic but in reality I don't think he would have enjoyed the day. And when we do finally get married, I need to know Sam is one hundred percent happy.

I know it's possible it might never happen. That's a risk I'm willing to take. I know that whether we do or we don't, it won't change our relationship. Being Sam's wife can't make me love him more than I already do.

I kiss him again, lingeringly, the romance of the on-screen wedding and the midsummer magic taking hold of me.

"Get a room!" Sophie laughs.

"We're in *our* room, thank you very much," Sam chides his daughter. "If you don't like it, you can get out."

"Alright, touchy!" She laughs again but I've caught her looking at him, when she thinks nobody can see. Her face full of concern. Last weekend has worried her, too. And she's decided she will spend half of the summer in Cornwall, and half in Devon, which seems a generous and more than welcome compromise.

Ben, oblivious to all that we are missing, and bored by the wedding, which is not a patch on *Dinosaur Train*, pushes between us and kisses Sam too.

"I love you, Daddy."

"I love you too, little man."

Now it's my turn. "I love you, Mummy."

"I love you, too."

Sophie shuffles up next to Sam and we close the laptop, having seen the main part of the day and knowing that all is well for Shona and Paul. Now it's time to focus on us.

26

To our surprise, Julie and I have been invited to the grand opening of the Bay Hotel.

"I don't think I'll bother," I said.

"No, nor me."

"I'll be knackered from moving, anyway."

"And I'll be too exhausted from missing you."

Our moving date was set for September, which had given Sam time to get out of plaster and up on his feet again. Nevertheless, he's not fully recovered, and we had plenty of offers of help from our friends and family, which we happily accepted.

It's been a bittersweet summer. So much has happened. Mum and Dad had their first fully-booked high season, and are subsequently shattered but triumphant and already planning for next year, with plenty of repeat bookings to help them maintain their confidence. Meanwhile, Jonathan has agreed to give living in Spain a try. Janie will support them financially at first but is confident he will find work quickly ("As long as you brush up on your A-Level Spanish, you'll be fine.") He has handed in his notice at Amethi but I think that Julie is pleased as she is now free to come back full-time; a return to how things began, while Luke has left his London days behind and is looking after Zinnia two days a week and she will be joining Ben at Goslings on the other three days.

"I'm so excited to be coming back, Alice," Julie told me. "And I feel bad saying this, after all that time of being desperate to be pregnant, but I don't think I'd have another child. I don't know. Maybe I'll change my mind. I love, love, love being a mum and I'd lay down my life for Zinnia, you know that. But god, it changes your life, doesn't it? And you know what? I've really missed working."

"I know exactly what you mean," I said. "And I can't wait to have you back. But I bet something else comes along to change things again. Nothing ever stays still for long."

"It's not like you to be so pessimistic!"

"I don't necessarily mean something bad. Just… something."

"Well, let's make the most of it while we can, shall we?"

Jon and Janie are set to leave in October, not long before David and Martin are jetting off to the States. "I'm scared you won't come back," I've said to David. "I don't want you to go. We were meant to spend more time together as the kids got older. I was looking forward to it."

"And we will, I promise. This is just one year."

"It had better be."

I've had these upcoming departures on my mind, and I've been wondering what life will be like without Jonathan or David, but I know I'll be OK. And like I said to Julie, nothing ever stays still for long. Whether it's for the better or the worse, things won't stay the same. I know that well enough by now.

"Why don't we have a party?" Sam suggested. "Something to say thanks to everyone for their help when we move house… and to say bye to Janie, and Jon. And Martin and David, too."

"OK," I'd said, "but I don't know when we'll get the chance to arrange it. There's not much time, you know, between us moving in and them moving on."

"What about the week after we move? The Saturday night?"

"At our new house?" I'd asked doubtfully.

"Mm… maybe not. I don't want anyone else coming in and mucking it up!" Sam smiled. "What about the Mowhay? Could we do it there?"

"I don't know. There are the guests to think about. I don't want to disturb them."

"We wouldn't have to. And we could invite them, too! That should sweeten them up."

"I guess. I'll ask Julie."

"Great."

As it turned out, that was the same weekend as the Bay Hotel grand opening. Of course, everything had to happen at once.

"Let's do both," Julie said. "Have a Saturday off."

"But someone needs to be there to welcome the guests."

"Jon can do it. He'll be buggering off soon. Let's make the most of him while he's still here."

"OK…" I'd said. "I guess we could do both."

In all honesty, I really just wanted a weekend in our new home. There are boxes everywhere and aside from the unpacking, I just want a night in. To settle Ben into bed then snuggle up with Sam on our new settee, watch some TV, get to bed early. But I suppose there'll be time for that.

Julie calls round at eleven. "Get dressed up," she'd instructed me. "Let's show them what we're made of."

It feels weird, walking through town on a Saturday in a dress and sandals, not to mention child-free. On my weekends off, I'm normally mooching about in jeans or shorts and a t-shirt, usually with Ben hanging off one arm and Meg's lead in the other hand.

"Shall we go for a cheeky half?" Julie asks.

"Should we?" I am swept up in a sudden gust of mischief.

"Yes! How often do we get time to do something like that, these days? Let's do it, for old times' sake!"

"OK… I'm in!"

It's still so warm, it could be the height of summer. But with schools back, it's not quite as hectic as July and August have been. Now, the town is swamped with older holidaymakers, as well as families with very young children. Julie and I manage to find a seat outside the Mainbrace and I go inside to get the drinks.

"Cheers!" Julie says, raising her glass.

"Cheers," I raise mine in answer. "To the Bay Hotel…"

"Failing miserably!" Julie finishes and we both laugh a little too meanly.

"We both know it's going to be a major success," I say.

"Yeah, probably."

We sit, happy and content, soaking up the September sun and watching the steady stream of people meandering past. On the harbour beach, families sit in the warmth, wriggling bare toes in the damp sand and sipping from takeaway cups. It feels so good to have this rare opportunity to sit here, leisurely, like we're on holiday ourselves. It's been a long time, or so it feels.

"Julie," I say.

"Yes?"

"I hope I have said this before but just in case I haven't, thank you. For everything. For being my best friend, and for persuading me to move down here."

To my surprise, ready tears spring to my friend's eyes. "Bloody hell, Alice. Don't make me cry. You've nothing to thank me for – at least nothing more than I should be thanking you for."

"But you know what I mean. You know I'd still be at World of bloody Stationery now if it wasn't for you!"

"No you wouldn't!"

"I might. Who knows? But I wouldn't be here, and I wouldn't have Sam, and Ben, and Soph, and…" Now my eyes are filling with tears as well.

Julie puts her hand on mine. "I think it's all happened as it was meant to."

"I like that idea."

"Now stop crying. You're ruining my street cred."

I laugh and wipe my eyes, and we return to our separate, quiet contemplation, utterly at ease with one another.

Once our glasses are empty, we rise from our seats, which are quickly filled by a couple who have been hanging around like the gulls who parade the harbour, ever-watchful for unguarded ice-creams or carelessly clutched pasties.

We seem to be walking against the general flow of people and have to dodge between hand-holding couples, dogs on leads and pushchairs. We make it up to the Bay Hotel safely and stop to get our breath, straightening each other's clothes and hair before we go in.

"It won't do to look any less than our best," Julie says. She pulls the thick embossed card invite from her bag and presents it to the doorman. A doorman! Imagine. I don't believe there has ever before been such a thing at a hotel in this town.

He smiles and opens the door for us. We walk into a highly polished lobby, where Lydia stands, tall and stunning as ever. She has had her hair cut and straightened and she's wearing what might be called a cocktail dress.

"Hello, Alice. Hi, Julie," she says sheepishly, her confidence seeming to drain momentarily. "I'm so glad you came. I didn't know if you would, after…"

"Of course we would!" I say, keen to cut her off and not be reminded of that awful weekend.

"Anything for a free drink," Julie says cheekily, accepting a glass from a black-shirted waiter.

I shoot her a warning glance. "We hope it goes really well, Lydia." I take a glass, too, and raise it to her. "All the best. I mean it."

"Thank you," she smiles. "Really."

Beneath that glossy, expensive haircut and the veneer of expensive clothes and make-up, I know she's the same Lydia she always was. Or maybe I'm a soft touch. But I have a real fondness for her, and admiration, too.

As another couple of guests come in, Lydia's attention turns to them and Julie and I walk through to the main dining area, where Felicity, in full evening dress despite it being late morning, is talking loudly and animatedly to a handful of people gathered around her. She casts a glance our way, looks us up and down, but clearly doesn't merit us as interesting or important enough to greet.

I recognise a chef from the TV and I nudge Julie. "I wonder if they've got him cooking here."

"To think they were after Jonathan! Having said that, I hadn't heard any rumours about a C-list chef coming to town so perhaps he's just one of Flic's mates."

We wander over to the floor-to-ceiling windows. There is a staggering, uninterrupted view across the sea. Today, it is as exquisitely turquoise as the Mediterranean and basking gently in the sun like a lazy cat. I know there will be other days, though, when it will be grey and wild and unruly, leaping at the windows, sending salt splatters across the glass and impenetrable mist to obscure the view. No matter how much somebody might spend to stay in this place, their money can't guarantee how the weather and sea behave.

There are a couple of canoeists not far from the rocks, tracing the shoreline, and I think momentarily that I'd like to switch places with them – feel the freedom of being out on the water, rather than the constriction of my dress and the confines of the hotel. I have to hand it to Lydia and Felicity, though. This place is stunning. And yes, maybe they do offer some of the same things that we do at Amethi, but really, this is in a different league. And I am happy for it to be so.

There will no doubt be rumblings of disapproval, amongst some of the locals, about this changing the tone of the town. And I can just imagine the crowd that will begin to come here. Wealthy Londoners, like Felicity. Semi-celebrities, like the chef who is currently looking longingly at Julie. Over-confident, loud and showy. Not all of them, of course. But I feel thoroughly satisfied that this place won't be taking any of Amethi's custom. The two places couldn't be more different.

We stay for an hour or so, but I can sense Julie doesn't really want to be here. She keeps looking at her watch.

"Am I boring you?"

"What? Oh, yes. Of course you are. You always do. No, sorry, it's just Luke said he'd bring Zinnie to pick us up and he'll give us a lift to Amethi, if you want to jump in with us."

"Erm, OK. Let me speak to Sam, though, in case he's waiting for me to go home first."

I walk through the huge open doorway onto the balcony, the gentle wind skimming across the top of the sea and over the rocks, playing with my hair and my skirt – another good reason to stick to trousers.

I hold my dress in place with one hand, holding the phone with the other. I call Sam and wait. I'm expecting it to go to voicemail when he answers. "Hi!"

"Hello. Are you OK? You sound out of breath."

"Oh, yeah, you know… just shifting furniture around."

"I said not to do that without me! You'll end up doing yourself a mischief," I smile, knowing that turn of phrase will make him laugh, too.

"It's fine," he says. "It has to be done."

"Oh, yeah, I know, but we could do it together tomorrow. It can wait. I can't imagine Ben's helping much!"

"No, it's OK. Mum's got Ben."

"Has she?" This is news to me.

"Yeah, just for an hour or so."

"Oh, OK. Well, we're going to leave here soon. Julie's going straight up to Amethi, and said she could give me a lift. But maybe I'd better come back home and we can go up together. I can help with any heavy lifting, if you absolutely insist it has to happen today."

What about the party? I want to ask. It was his idea but he's hardly put any thought into how it's all going to happen.

"No, don't worry. Aren't you all dressed up, anyway? You don't want to come back here and get hot and sweaty. You go up with Julie and I'll meet you there."

"OK. I'll see you in a bit. An hour or so? We'd better make sure everything's ready for later."

"It will be. I've got it under control, I promise."

I'm not convinced.

Before we leave, I go to the bathroom, which is predictably swanky, with highly polished tiles, expensive soap and hand cream. I return to find Julie waiting in the lobby, looking more than ready to go. We head out into the sunshine, thanking the smiling doorman as he lets us through. I'm surprised by the relief I feel to be out of there.

Luke is already waiting, and I climb into the back next to Zinnia, who is strapped into her car seat, shovelling raisins into her mouth.

"Luke!" Julie says, "I said not to let her get anything on that dress!"

"It is a nice dress," I say, admiring it. "Are you all ready for the party, Zinnie?"

She smiles, waving her arm and distributing the remaining raisins across me.

"Now look!" says Julie. "They're all over Alice's dress."

"It's fine! We're fine aren't we, Zinnia?"

Luke and Julie exchange a look and we head out of town, me feeling like a second child in the back of their car.

As we approach Amethi, I can see Mum and Dad's car is parked up. I'm sure I said to come mid-afternoon. I suppose they can help get the place set up. Sam's obviously rushed up, too, as his car is parked next to theirs. Good. I was starting to feel a bit annoyed that he wasn't putting any effort into this party. I know it's like a busman's holiday for Julie and me, organising something like this, but that's not the point, really. It was Sam's idea. I check my irritation. I'm just tired, from the move, and I think I'm still really getting over Sam's accident and the effect that's had on our lives.

He's here now, I tell myself. *Get over it, Alice. It's a party. It's meant to be fun.*

Luke plucks Zinnia from her car seat and Julie holds the seat forward for me as I climb out. "Here," she brushes me down. "Sorry about the raisins." She plucks one from my hair and straightens it then pulls me into a huge hug.

"It's OK. You know I'm used to it with Ben." I pull back. I'm sure she's shaking slightly. "Julie, are you alright?"

"I'm fine," she smiles breezily. "Honestly."

"OK." I can tell she doesn't want to talk about it now. I make a mental note to quiz her later, when the party's in full swing. Maybe we can have a few quiet moments.

Julie squeezes my arm, and takes my hand. "Come on," she says, and we walk together across the gravel.

It's not easy in heels, even though mine are a minimal height. I think as I often do how women's clothes seem to be designed to put them at a disadvantage. No running or climbing in skirts and heels. The more cynical among us might think it's to prevent us getting away from men.

As we round the corner, I see my dad. "You're a bit early!" I scold him.

"I know. Sorry, love." He kisses my cheek. "You look nice."

"You don't look too bad yourself!" He's in a suit; a rare thing for him. "Don't you think you're going to get a bit hot in that, though?"

"Oh, I'll be fine."

"I'll just be a sec," Julie says, scurrying off round the corner.

"OK," I call lamely as Dad launches into some waffle about the new flowers he's put in the window boxes at the Sail Loft. "They should look great, Alice, they're meant to flower all the way through winter. I thought they'd look nice up here, too, what do you think? Outside those windows there," he turns me to look at the windows in the courtyard.

"Yeah, that sounds nice, Dad, if you've got some spare. We'd better go and get things sorted for this party right now, though. I'll have a look at the window boxes next time I'm at the Sail Loft."

"OK," Dad says. "You're right, we'd better get moving. Come on, Alice. This party isn't going to organise itself."

We walk together towards the Mowhay. It's beautifully still at Amethi right now. A fluttering of jackdaws rises from the line of trees, cackling as they lift into the air and rearrange themselves before descending once more. The air still hums with insects, too; the wildflower meadows now golden in the sun, soon to be stripped of their glory and cut down to settle over winter, ready to rise again.

Outside the Mowhay, all the furniture looks like it's been cleaned, and the tables are set with glasses and shining glass jugs ready to be filled, standing next to centrepieces of beautiful flower displays.

"Who's done all this?" I gasp. "It's beautiful. Was it you and Mum? Is that why you got here so early?"

"No," Dad says. "This was all Sam."

"Really?" Last time I spoke to Sam, he was lumping furniture around at home. How has he managed to do all this?

The bifold doors are open to the elements and the sun is bright behind the Mowhay so I am dazzled for a moment but then, as my eyes adjust to the light, all becomes clear.

The room has been set out with two rows of chairs, facing the outside. On these rows of chairs sit most of the people I love most in the world. Nearly all of them. Not Sam. Not Dad. Not Luke.

Because there are Sam and Luke, in suits, standing next to the open doorway and looking at me – Luke smiling, Sam very serious. And there, standing next to them, is Lizzie. She is smiling at me, too. I hold onto Dad's arm.

"Oh no…" I say.

"Oh yes." He turns to me now, allowing a tear to drop from his eyelashes. He kisses my cheek and I hear him swallow a sob, as he leads me to where Sam and Luke are standing. Julie, just behind, is in floods of tears and she hands a bouquet to Zinnia, who totters towards me, smiling shyly. I'm in shock. But I take the flowers. "Thank you, Zinnie," I say, as though this was the most normal thing in the world.

I look at Sam and he holds out his hand. I see Mum smiling widely at me, holding Ben close to her. She's not much of a crier, my mum. It's Dad who's the emotional one. Nevertheless, she is beaming and if I'm not much mistaken her eyes do look slightly more shiny than normal.

I take Sam's hand and I realise I am shaking. He is, too.

"OK?" he asks.

"Yes, I… I think so!" I'm crying now too. "Is this real?"

"Yes," he says. "This is real. And I hope you don't mind that I've sprung it on you like this."

"Do I mind…? I don't think so." The words stutter out. "But is it even allowed? I mean, we're not licensed for…"

"You're right. You're not. But don't ruin the romance! It is real, but it's not exactly standard. We'll have to do it legally at the registry office but forget all that for now. It may not be official but this is as real, and romantic, and true as it gets!"

I look along the row of chairs. Mum and Dad and Ben; Karen and Ron; Julie and Zinnia; Janie and Jonathan; Kate, Isaac, Sophie and Jacob; David, Martin, Esme and Tyler; Christian and Sadie; Luke's dad, Jim; Julie's mum, Cherry, and Julie's brother, Lee. All the people who would have come to our original wedding. All looking at me and Sam and smiling their encouragement.

I turn back to Sam, then to Lizzie. "Hello."

"Hello!" she laughs. "Would you like to begin?"

"More than anything."

"I thought you hated *Don't Tell the Bride*!" I say to Sam as we stand in front of the meadow, having our photos taken.

"I do! But none of this was for TV, was it? And also, I didn't have to choose your dress and risk a total meltdown."

"No wonder Julie was so bothered about Zinnia chucking raisins all over me!"

"I'd marry you in anything. Or in nothing. In fact, I quite like that idea…"

"Sam!" I say. "The photographer might hear."

"Ah well, I'm sure he's heard much worse." Sam turns to me and pulls me to him, kissing me fervently. "Here, let's give him something to really work with."

I feel like I'm in a dream. I'm certainly dazed and everywhere I look I'm amazed to find how much work has been put into today, without me suspecting a thing.

Together, Julie and Jonathan have made a huge feast that would feed three times as many people as are here.

"But this is meant to be your party!" I say to Jon. "Your leaving party."

"Is it, though?" He grins.

"Oh, I see what you mean. No, I suppose that was just to put me off the scent, wasn't it?"

"Er… yeah."

"Sorry, I'm being a bit dense."

"That's OK, Alice. I'm just glad you were happy about it. I had this horrible vision of you turning up and not wanting any of this, at all."

"Are you kidding? It's just… beautiful. And you've all worked so hard."

"David and Martin sorted all the drinks. Sam did the flowers, with a bit of help from your mum. Paul and Shona paid for the food…"

"No way!"

"Yes way. They felt bad about stealing your big day."

"And they're not even here…"

"No, they said they didn't expect to be invited and were just happy to be able to help this happen for you. But they might come up for a drink later."

"They must!" I exclaim. "Bloody hell." I am crying again.

Jonathan puts his arms round me. "You deserve it, Alice. You and Sam."

"I'm going to miss you so much, Jon. But I hope life only gets better for you now."

"It will, I will make sure it does. And I'll be back, you know. You can't get rid of me that easily."

With the autumn sun low in the sky, casting shadows across the ground, I sit with Mum and Dad.

"Happy?" Mum asks.

"Yes. Thank you. Very."

"We're only sorry you can't have a honeymoon yet," Dad says, offering me a glass of wine. I hold my hand up. I don't want to drink a thing. I want to remember every detail of this beautiful day. I pour a glass of water instead.

"I love you so much," Mum says and her eyes glisten.

"You're crying!" I exclaim triumphantly.

"Alice," Dad says, "that's not very nice."

"But Mum never cries! I'd have been disappointed if she didn't, on her daughter's wedding day." I hug her tightly. "I love you so much, too."

Karen comes to join us, and Ron. I feel very close to him since that night in June. And a little in awe of him as well, if I'm honest.

"Congratulations, Alice," he raises his glass to me.

"Thank you," I smile. Karen, half-cut – no longer as used to alcohol as she once was – slurs, "I'm so happy, Alice, that you and Sam found each other."

"Thanks, Karen," I stand and hug her. "I am, too. And I'm really glad that you're back in Cornwall. Honestly."

We look at each other. There is no point in being disingenuous; I didn't always feel this way and we both know it. But now, I would hate it if she left. Luckily, she seems to have struck gold with Ron. I hope they continue to be happy together.

Tyler, Esme, Ben, Zinnia and Jacob dash around between the tables, giggling and shouting and occasionally falling out with each other but quickly making up again, with occasional adult intervention. Really, this could be any day for them. They're just happy to be outdoors, running around in the sun.

I see Julie watching her daughter proudly. As full of life and fun as her mum, once Zinnia got moving, there was no stopping her.

"Excuse me a moment," I say, standing and chasing after the kids, laughing. Trying to grasp that childlike feeling of freedom, if only for a moment.

"Our two are going to miss Ben and Zinnie," Martin says, when I've admitted defeat and stopped for a rest.

"They'll all miss each other. And I'll miss you so much, you and David."

"We will be back, you know. I mean, I'm looking forward to the States, and it will be really good for David to see Bea, but my family's all here. And you're part of David's family too, you know, Alice. You and Sam and Ben. But I know things will have changed again by the time we're back. Nothing stays the same for long with you lot, does it?"

239

"No," I say. "You're very wise, Martin."

"I wish you'd tell David that!"

"My ears are burning!" David appears behind us, putting an arm round each of us. "Were you talking about how amazing I am?"

"What else?" I smile. "While you're both here, I wanted to thank you for all this. Jon said you've bought all the drinks for today. And there was I thinking it was a farewell party for you, and for him and Janie."

"I just can't believe you fell for it," David grins. "You're even dimmer than I thought you were."

"Thanks for that. I was just saying how much I'm going to miss you but I think I've changed my mind…"

"I'm going to miss you, Alice, like you wouldn't believe. But I'm so excited about seeing Bea. She was extremely jealous she couldn't be here today."

"Give her and Bob my love, won't you?"

"Yes, of course."

When the evening sun has disappeared behind the line of trees, the darkness brings a handful of new guests to the party: Paul & Shona; Cindy our amazing housekeeper and her husband, Rod; Lizzie's boyfriend Med; Sarah, and her twins, who waste no time in joining the other kids who are still running about like mad things, fuelled by home-made lemonade and wedding cake.

Sam lights a fire and we pull the tables and chairs round so that we can all stay warm. There are an awful lot of empty beer and wine bottles by now, and more than one wide-mouthed yawn, but there also seems to be a general reluctance to bring the day to a close. I feel it, too. I never want this to end, although at the same time I would also like to have my husband to myself.

"Come for a walk?" I suggest to him and we stand, and slip quietly away, hand in hand. We skirt along the edge of the wildflower meadow, towards the woods. I find it hard to believe how short a time it is since I happened across Jonathan there. And how life has turned again for him.

"Sam," I say.

He stops and turns to me. "Yes?"

"Thank you. For everything."

"Alice. You have nothing to thank me for. You've kept me going this year and I know I've been a miserable git at times."

"I hadn't noticed," I smile, squeezing his hand and turning him to face me. I kiss his soft, shaven cheek.

He laughs. "Honestly, I'm just so grateful for all of this," he gestures towards our friends and family. "I don't know if I'll ever feel happier than I do right now. Not just getting married but knowing all these people love us. I feel like we've got this unbreakable wall of support."

"I know what you mean."

"And I feel like… no, I know… if you hadn't come back into my life, things would be so different now. Who knows what would have happened with Mum? If she'd come back and you'd not been here."

"You'd have sorted it out."

"I'm grateful for your faith in me." In the dark it's hard to tell but I think he's close to tears. "But I'm not sure I would. I held onto a lot of bitterness, for a long time. But you helped me release some of that. And now I've got Mum, and Janie, back – even if Janie's buggering off to Spain again – and you're so great with Sophie, and you've given me… you've given me Ben…"

He's definitely crying now. I pull him softly towards me. "You've missed someone."

"Who…? Oh, Meg. Of course. I can't forget Meg."

"You're right, though I didn't mean her, actually. I take his hand gently and I move it to my stomach.

He looks at me, his eyes searching my face for confirmation. "You mean…?"

"Yes." I pull back a little so I can see him properly. Check that he looks happy. "I've been a bit slow on the uptake. I've felt weird for ages; even that weekend, back in June, when… well, you know. Then with everything that's been going on, it didn't even occur to me. Not until this week. I popped to the chemist this morning. I did the test at the toilet in the Bay Hotel! I couldn't wait any longer."

"Oh my god. I think my heart's going to burst. How is it possible to feel so happy?"

"I don't know," I say, kissing him tenderly. "But I feel the same. Let's not tell anyone else yet, shall we? Keep this little secret between us for now."

Sam nods and he kisses me back, long and slow. I close my eyes and focus on the feel of his lips on mine. So comfortable, so familiar, and so completely right.

The chatter and laughter of our family and friends carries across the field. My heart swells at the thought of them all. Above us, the leaves rustle contentedly in the slight breeze. Already, they are starting to turn to gold, the occasional castaway spiralling slowly to the ground.

There is a shuffling in the undergrowth; a hedgehog, maybe, or a mouse. In the branches above, an owl calls into the darkness of the night. Its call is answered somewhere not too far away.

Sam holds me close and I slip my arms around his waist; lay my head against his chest; listen to the steady, reassuring beat of his heart. He is solid, and strong, and warm, this man. The love of my life. The father of my children. My husband. I never want to let him go.

The first six Coming Back to Cornwall books:

All books are available as paperbacks and
ebooks, online and in store.
Contact **katharine@heddonpublishing.com** for
further information.

Acknowledgements

As you may be aware, as I've certainly mentioned it more than once, the Coming Back to Cornwall series was originally intended to be a trilogy. I added two further books, convinced that I'd end it at book five (*Lighting the Sky*) but in the strangeness of 2020 I found myself back here again! It's been a year of stress and sadness for many people, through two lockdowns and fear about the virus that's been sweeping the world. In my family, we have lost my mum and my mother-in-law, both to cancer, and I've found it comforting to carry on writing about Alice and Sam and to give them a happy ending, which I hope you will have enjoyed. In a time of anxiety, why not escape into something happier, for a while at least? It's been such a pleasure hearing from readers who've enjoyed these books this year. It's definitely helped me to write them.

As always, I owe a huge debt of gratitude to all the people who have supported me through the process of writing and producing this book. Fellow author Nelly Harper, for her detailed feedback and incredibly helpful knowledge about all things pagan. I love writing about the solstice celebrations, and wish I could actually be a part of them.

I would also like to thank Niki Brooks at the St Ives RNLI, who has kindly given her time to educate me on the training and practice of the lifeboat crews. I've long admired the people who volunteer for the RNLI and it was a real eye-opener talking to Niki and finding out more about how it all works.

Special thanks also to Hilary Kerr, for her excellent proofreading skills and editing advice. And to my dad, Ted

Rogers, for the same. Three pairs of eyes are definitely better than one (as long as they're the right pairs of eyes).

As ever, thank you to my amazing team of beta readers, who have given me fantastic feedback to bear in mind as I've worked my way back through the book. I'm so grateful to people for giving their time to do this and I am always worried I will forget somebody at this point. Huge thanks to Katie Copnall, Julie Mitchell, Beryl Gibson, Yvonne Carpenter, Sandra Francis, Pat Lawes, Barbara Parkin, Joanna Blackburn, Jude Wolfe, Holly Reeves, Jean Crowe, Claire Ingram, Kate Jenkins, Claudia Baker, and Rosalyn Osborn. I'd also like to say a special thanks to Gill Corbett for her friendship and keeping me in a Cornish frame of mind this year! I really have missed coming down to Cornwall this year but hopefully that means next time will be all the more special.

The dedication to this book is to my family, and this includes every one of them. My children, Laura and Edward; my husband, Chris; my parents, Rosemary and Ted Rogers, and my brothers, John and Richard – their wives, Deborah and Jules, and my excellent nephews and niece, Owen, Daniel, Stan, and Emily. My parents-in-law, Kaye and Barry Smith, and my brother- and sister-in-law, Stewart and Vickie Smith, and niece Harriet.

All my uncles and aunts, cousins, and their families. The list really does go on and long may it continue. You have all been such a huge support this year and I know we're all sharing the sadness. I'm so very grateful and proud to be part of this family, and I consider myself incredibly lucky.

In memory of Mum and Kaye, I am looking forward to better, brighter days for us all.

Also by Katharine E. Smith:

Writing the Town Read - Katharine's first novel.

"I seriously couldn't put it down and would recommend it to anyone to doesn't like chick lit, but wants a great story."

Looking Past - a story of motherhood, and growing up without a mother.

"Despite the tough topic the book is full of love, friendships and humour. Katharine Smith cleverly balances emotional storylines with strong characters and witty dialogue, making this a surprisingly happy book to read."

Amongst Friends - a back-to-front tale of friendship and family, set in Bristol.

"An interesting, well written book, set in Bristol which is lovingly described, and with excellent characterisation. Very enjoyable."

CPSIA information can be obtained
at www.ICGtesting.com
Printed in the USA
BVHW031321180321
602899BV00009B/117

9 781913 166366